Tails of a Country Vet

Abbott "Pete" Smith, D.V.M.

Gina McKnight
Illustrations by Kelly Lincoln

Monday Creek Publishing
Ohio USA

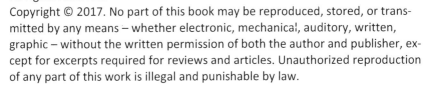

1. Smith, Abbott P.   2. Veterinarian – Ohio – Athens 3. Veterinary medicine – Ohio – Athens   4. Veterinary medicine - Equine

Monday Creek Publishing | P.O. Box 399 | Buchtel, Ohio USA
mondaycreekpublishing.com

On the Front Cover
Top Right: 1949. Pete Smith, 11 years, riding in Maine.
Bottom Right: 1958. Pete Smith riding Witezar in Colorado.
Top Right: Pete Smith, D.V.M. during surgery at Milliron Clinic
Bottom Right: Pete Smith, D.V.M. preparing for surgery at Milliron Clinic.

ISBN-10: 978-0692898260
ISBN-10: 0692898263

For Pat

Foreword

Abbott "Pete" Smith, D.V.M. was an icon in southeastern Ohio for many years. Raised in Maine, a cowboy in Colorado, then finally to Ohio and his own Milliron Clinic, Dr. Smith will remain part of the Ohio Valley that he loved. This book is a testimony to his commitment to life – from the physical state of a wounded animal, to the emotional connection pets play in our daily lives. Through his decades in veterinary practice, Dr. Smith realized the impact of animals - how they enrich relationships, enhance our perceptions, and nurture our spirituality.

An honor roll member of the American Veterinary Medical Association, Ohio Veterinary Medical Association, and the Athens County Chapter of the Ohio Horseman's Council, Dr. Smith served his community through miraculous surgeries, words of wisdom, and robust living. From his arrival to Ohio in 1963, to his unexpected death in 2010, we marvel, revere, and celebrate Dr. Smith's life.

Interviewing hundreds of Dr. Smith's clients, I found a common thread – a valued relationship between a pet owner and their vet. In *Tails of a Country Vet*, I present to you many hours of transcription, emails, and letters from Dr. Smith's clients and staff. Whether they make you giggle, wince, furrow your brow, or remain contemplative, all the stories to follow are heartfelt and sincere. It is an intimate journey into the lives of pets and humans.

Thank you to the people who contributed to this book. It was fun meeting you, hearing your story and feeling your compassion for Dr. Smith. Special thanks to Dr. Smith's family – Jody, Jessica, and Pat.

Gina McKnight

Introduction

Welcome to Milliron Clinic, Athens, Ohio, USA. Traveling to Milliron Clinic from US Route 33 South to the State Route 550 exit, you will encounter rolling foothills fanning from the Appalachian Mountains. Driving along the two-lane road, several small burghs snuggle parallel to the banks of Sugar Creek. Finally, on the right-hand side of the road, the iconic sign "Milliron Clinic: Abbott P. Smith, D.V.M." comes into view.

Turning south, the rumble of the cattleguard signifies that you have officially entered Milliron Farm and Clinic. To the left flies the Milliron flag. Created by employee and artist Kelly Lincoln, the flag's blue background is offset by the Milliron Brand. Sycamore trees grove to the right of the clinic, just beyond the bridge over the McDougal Branch of Federal Creek. The road to the farmhouse is just ahead, up the steep hill, beyond the oak plank fence that surrounds the facility.

The clinic stands to the left of the bridge; regal with its variegated orange ombre` brick, proprietary stables, and surgical facilities. Clicker-training dog agility articles can be seen to the side of the barn, as well as the vast supply of firewood for the clinic's woodstove.

Entering the clinic through the glass door, you'll find the art of Shary B. Akers, a former Ohio University student who painted the large mural of Milliron Farm. Depicted in the mural are the animals Pete and Jody brought with them from Colorado, and some acquired after their arrival; Persimmon, the grey jenny; Lollipop, the black jenny; Silver Dollar, the pony; Poo 2, the seal-point Siamese cat; Jody's German shepherd, Shane; Melody, Pete's coonhound; Tinker Toy, Jessica's Shetland pony; Cricket, Pete's mare; and Jody's beloved gelding Starboy. The local McDougal Church stands in the background amidst the rolling hills. The floor to ceiling mural captures the essence of the Smith family; their love of animals, their passion for art, and their commitment to community.

The smell of combiotic mingled with Clorox bleach fill the reception area. Sitting on ochre tile floors are church pews for clients and pets to wait. Across from the church pews is the counter where the receptionist greets clients, answers questions, and keeps the daily schedule. Behind the reception desk are drawers upon drawers of client's files.

The reception counter wraps around to the animal scale, where animals are weighed upon arrival. To the left of the scale is the woodstove, two examination rooms, and another seating area. On the knotty pine wall proudly hangs the Moravian Creed along with Dr. Smith's trademark, the Milliron Brand.

The aquarium that is encased in the reception counter holds the interest of children and adults alike as they wait in the reception area. Through the years, the tank contained several species of fish, including goldfish, catfish, and alligator gar.

The door to the kennels is to the left of the reception desk. Barking dogs and mewing cats greet your entrance into the belly of the clinic. Kennels are arranged from floor to ceiling and contain animals recovering from surgery and those awaiting treatment. A nearby table is where animals are prepped for surgery and sedation. A few of the tables came from Army surplus, while others are high-dollar surgical steel. There are shelves of bandages, syringes, and other important vetting instruments. Vet techs are busy working on small dogs and cats; cleaning teeth, clipping nails, and replacing soiled bandages. Down the hall is what used to be the furnace room, but is now the laundry room. Next is the darkroom for developing X-rays, and then forward to the large surgical area, leading to the surgical preparation room, the clinic stables, and more kennels.

Outside, the parking lot sometimes fills completely, with no room to turn around. Mega horse trailers, lowboys, stock trailers, shabby trailers, and many more, all have made a mark on the gravel and square drainage outlets that dot the parking lot. The clinic cats like to jump in car windows and pee in the interior, but the peacocks remain the guardians of the outer limits.

Now that you've arrived at Milliron Clinic, meet Dr. Smith, his patients, clients, animals, and family (Jody, his wife; Jessica, his daughter; and Pat, his son). We invite you to a place where miracles occur on a regular basis, souls find comfort, wisdom is eagerly shared, and pets sometimes find the rainbow bridge.

Abbott "Pete" Smith, D.V.M.

Table of Contents

Abbott "Pete" Smith, D.V.M.

Grand Canyon Gerty

Suzanne Rozzo

Pete had a soft spot for mules. It was 7 p.m., time for equine appointments. The clinic parking lot was full of horse trailers, everything from homemade trailers that rattled down the road to expensive rigs with gold trimmings. There were no set appointments; it was horses at 7 p.m. for everyone. Dr. Smith had an idea ahead of time which clients were coming and the problems they were having with their equines. I arrived first with my mule Gunsmoke. Pretty soon people were out of their trucks and they were all standing by their horse trailers. They had their show horses and I am standing there with my little mule. One of the guys with a fancy rig looks over at me. I am standing by myself and he says real crass, "Is that mule gaited?" I just looked at him and made a face. He looked at me like, "*What the hell are you doing with that thing*?" Then he turned his back on me.

It was my first time at Milliron Clinic. I was thinking, *what am I doing? I don't know*. Then out from the barn came this man who I thought was the tractor mechanic; his green coveralls and his glasses down over his nose. He walks up and looks around at all the horses, points at me and says, "Bring that mule in here!"

I thought, *"Oh! Me? The tractor mechanic?"* Then I realized it was Dr. Smith. I looked over my shoulder at the others and thought, *"Um huh..."* In we went.

Once inside the clinic, Dr. Smith grabbed Gunsmoke by the throat right away. He's holding onto her throat and looking her all over. He's asking me all these questions about what I know about her. I told him that I just got her and this thing in her throat had been vet checked, but I wanted another opinion. He never let go of her throat. I said that I just had a young fellow come out and he trimmed her feet. I told Dr. Smith that the guy had said that my mule had foundered on all four. Dr. Smith whipped around and looked at me and said, "Mules don't founder!"

With a quick nod of his head, Dr. Smith yanked a pocket knife out of his pocket and lifted her foot. Stuff was flying everywhere. He put her foot down and said, "She's not foundered. There's a little bit of thrush in there from not getting cleaned right. Leave her. I'll clean her feet the way they should be cleaned and I'll take this thing out of her throat. Pick her up tomorrow."

I looked at my husband and my husband looks at me. We were thinking... *Well...* I asked, "Pick her up tomorrow? How much is this going to cost?"

Dr. Smith looked at Gunsmoke's throat again, then looked at her feet and gave me a price for his services. I said, "Well, Dr. Smith, do you think I am crazy for spending that kind of money on this animal?"

Dr. Smith whipped around and looked at me and said, "Can you think of the enjoyment you are going to get out of riding this animal? Leave her. Pick her up tomorrow. I'll take that thing out of her throat and clean her feet. Pick her up tomorrow." He took the mule and we walked out of the clinic.

When we arrived at the clinic the next day, Gunsmoke had some tubes sticking out of her. Dr. Smith said everything went right and that it was something that he had never seen; it was a cyst on her thyroid. He said it was a dead cyst. I wish that I could have seen it. Her feet looked like he had taken a hatchet to them. It was like she was standing on these little balls. Dr. Smith said he got all of the thrush out of her feet and to keep them clean. He said she would be fine. We got her out of the stall and took her home.

One day we returned to the clinic with Gunsmoke. We talked with Dr. Smith about our recent trip to the Grand Canyon. We told him about the time we rode mules through the canyon. He was very interested in our adventure and said he always wanted to ride a mule through the Grand Canyon. From that day forward, whenever he saw Gunsmoke, he would say in his Dr. Smith voice, "How's Grand Canyon Gerty?"

Butch

Susan Blackford

When I lived in northern Ohio I rescued pets, taking in strays. I moved to the Athens, Ohio, area where I met Dr. Smith, it was over thirty-three years ago. Because I rescued and took in so many strays over the years, and had very little money to work with, Pete always came up with workable, cheap home remedies.

One time I brought a badly injured rescue dog who needed a very complicated surgery to Milliron Clinic. Dr. Smith asked, "Why did you bring this dog to me?" I replied, "Because you are the best there is and that's what he needs." Pete smiled and went to work. The dog had been mangled to the point of possibly losing all four legs. Pete was able to save all four, and the dog recovered completely.

Pete always enjoyed a good surgical challenge. The harder

the challenge, the more creative Pete's brain would get. He would assess the problem and come up with his own miracle inventions to save his patients.

Of all the dogs I brought to Pete, the story of Butch is the most memorable. A friend and neighbor of ours completed two tours in Vietnam. He was exposed to agent orange. He didn't have a lot of money to live on and was fighting cancer. Someone had dropped off three dogs to him. Butch was one of them. Once a month, we would take dog food and treats to our neighbor for Butch. This was made possible by the contributions of a wonderful local rescue group. We dropped off food and treats for two years. It has been over five years that our friend lost his final battle to cancer. A month before, he stopped by our house. He said, "Susie, if something should happen to me, would you see to my dogs?" I said, "Sony, you don't even have to ask." When we arrived at his home to pick up his dogs, Butch was on the floor – dying. Our friend had been too sick to realize that Butch had been run over and badly crushed. We took Butch to Dr. Smith.

Upon arrival at Milliron Clinic, I told Dr. Smith Butch's sad story. Dr. Smith operated and Butch healed nicely. Dr. Smith wrote the following letter to me after the surgery:

Butch is a wonderful dog. He is recovering from

devastating injuries to both hind legs, back and pelvis. In November, he had surgery to remove the femoral head from both femurs and I plated his pelvis. He is recovering well, and should continue to strengthen over the next several years.

At this time he needs to be kept indoors. He needs assistance with steps and getting in the car. He should not be tied out or on a line where he might become tangled. Use caution traversing slippery surfaces. He cannot roughhouse with other dogs or children. He should make a great companion to the home.

Pete Smith

Lucas and Lady

Mary Ann Chase

It's 9 a.m. and Dr. Pete Smith is walking down the hill from his home to his office. The parking lot is already stacked with cars loaded with small animals of all sorts and their owners of all sorts. Thus begins another routine day at Milliron Clinic, known and respected far and wide throughout Ohio and neighboring states. Dr. Pete never turned away any two-leggeds or four-leggeds. His heart knows no bounds.

All morning the small animals are treated. Meanwhile the parking lot is filling up with horse trailers from far and near. Is it any wonder that Dr. Pete has not time for farm calls? He is well-known to successfully perform major surgery on horses and small animals as well as treat all sorts of wounds, ailments, conditions of age and genetics, fractures and basic routine care. Is he able to trudge back up the hill to home by 9 p.m.? Not always. This is one very dedicated man, deeply loved and supported by wife Jody, children Pat and Jessica, grandchildren and thousands of grateful owners.

Several of my animals have benefited from Dr. Pete's expert care, and I hold dear many fond memories of those occasions. One day he was treating my beloved seventeen-year-old Australian shepherd Lucas while also working with my Tennessee Walker Lady. He said I could hangout backstage while he juggled my two, plus a clinic full of others. It was thrilling to watch Doc dash to and fro, checking Lucas' X-rays, doctoring Lady in the stall, returning to give Lucas a quick injection as he walked past. It was a frantic beehive of activity with Nanette, Annette, and his very competent staff assisting and reassuring us pet owners. I'll never forget that day as I was privilege to witness the drama up close and personal.

Later, Dr. Pete kindly and gently saw my Lucas and Lady through their final days with care and compassion. He even gave me a much appreciated hug to comfort me. As Lady was buried on the Milliron property, that spring I desired to see her final resting place. It was a very muddy day as I trudge east through the lumberyard to the location. On the way back, I chose a short-cut – my bad! The mud accumulated on my shoes so heavily that I had to scrape them with a stick every few steps. Ultimately, they were totally buried in ankle-deep mud, and I could do nothing other than to step out of those buried shoes and proceed all the way back in stocking feet! Fortunately, I didn't step on anything sharp. I was praying hard about it!

I told Dr. Pete not to worry if he later found a deserted pair of shoes - the owner survived. This little episode provided a welcome bit of humor into an otherwise sad occasion.

Just before Christmas holidays, Dr. Pete tended to a deep abscess in the right rear toe of my Thoroughbred Re-Pete. He invited me to watch as he sat down on an over-turned canister and cut deeply into the profusely bleeding hoof with strength and complete confidence. Meanwhile I was horrified at the silver dollar size hole in that hoof toe! But, Dr. Pete assured me this had to be done to get all the infection out. Then came my own dilemma – how to manage this wound. I so wanted to go home to Texas for Christmas, and there was no place for the care Re-Pete needed during the holidays. With tremendous generosity, Dr. Pete agreed to board him in the marvelous Milliron stable. The staff, as well as Jody, kept excellent care of Re-Pete for seven weeks. That horse continues sound today due to that top-of-the-line care.

Kazan
Merry Cibula

I have so many wonderful stories and memories of Pete dating back to the 70's when I worked for him for two years – best and *hardest* job I ever had! I learned so much every day!! One of my fondest memories was our staff meetings at Abdella's restaurant in Chauncey. Cathy, Nanette, Shelly, Jan, Jessica, of course Pete. I'm not sure how long the meetings lasted, but the dinner after was out of this world! What a treat!

I worked the evening shift, 3:00 p.m. to 9:00 p.m., or whenever Pete was done seeing horses, so I didn't see too much surgery as most of the surgeries were in the morning, but there were many nights when we had just finished with the horses, were cleaning up, and the phone would ring. Someone had a pet or horse emergency; could Pete see him? Of course, they lived an hour's drive away. Of course, Pete said, "Yes, bring him over." Sometimes we would end up in surgery until late into the night. I don't know where Pete found his energy, but his focus never wavered. We all drew from that energy and focus. We learned and grew from it.

One of my best memories of Pete involved my infamous dog "Kazan" who I brought from Africa after Peace Corps. Pete fondly referred to him as an "African Crusted Hound." Kazan had contracted venereal cancer. The only option, short of cancer drugs, was to put him down. I said my tearful goodbyes that morning and brought him into work, put him in a kennel, and waited for the inevitable call from Pete to bring him out. When he did, I asked, "Pete, isn't there anything else you can do for him?" Pete thought a minute, got on the phone to Ohio State University, just happened to get the expert on this particular disease on the phone and found out about a new treatment involving removing the tumor, making a vaccine out of it and injecting it back into the dog. So into surgery we went, and I am happy to say Kazan lived many, many years after that.

West Virginia Mare

Laura Gibson

I met Dr. Pete Smith through my farrier Jim Bonnett. I needed a veterinarian who could put my foal's ankle back together. My foal's mother had crushed it by stepping on it trying to keep another horse from coming too near her baby. At that time Pete was coming to our part of West Virginia once or twice a month. He would visit various stables and doctor their horses.

Pete came to our barn and checked my injured foal. He talked to my parents and said to bring the foal and his "lunch box" (the mare) to his clinic outside of Athens, Ohio, and he would see what he could do. My mother, brother, and I set out for Athens as soon as we could.

Once at Milliron Clinic, Pete examined the foal and planned for surgery to repair the foal's crushed ankle. Upon

Pete's recommendation, we left my foal and mare with Pete for a week.

When we went back to get them, my foal was in a cast up to his hock. He was to remain in the cast all summer. Pete explained that he had removed the crushed bone and literally pieced together the rest of the ankle with several screws. The ankle would mend. Other than the hoof being slightly more narrow than the others, the surgery was unnoticeable.

On two other occasions my horses had need of Pete's help. He removed a cancerous cyst from my favorite riding horse's chin and gelded the young stud that he had pieced together as a foal.

Since I had always had mares, I had never seen a stud gelded before. I was surprised and shocked when Pete simply sedated my horse, cut off the testicles, and tossed them to our family dog who quickly gobbled up both testicles. I've told this story many times and laugh as people I tell it to grimace and grip their thighs!

A good twenty years later, I was in need of Pete's gifted abilities again. A mare I had boarded for years, then purchased because of her good health and personality, had injured her front left hoof. From my kitchen window I noticed that she was favoring one of her front legs. When I went to see about it, I noticed she had torn the hoof from the coronet.

When I went to spray it off so that I could see it clearly, the hose water shot directly through the top of the hoof out the bottom of the hoof.

I immediately loaded her up and took her to the nearest veterinary clinic. X-rays were taken and doctors were consulted. I was told to take her to a hoof specialty clinic in Lexington, Kentucky. I went out to my truck and called Milliron Clinic and Pete said to bring her out. The next day, I did just that.

My mare was at Pete's for one week. He explained that he had removed approximately a one to two-inch square chunk off the top of her hoof. He also said that the area had smelled up the whole surgical area. Infection had already set in. He put her in a cast. I was told to bring her back in two months. Also, while he had my mare sedated, he removed a golf ball size cancer just at the throat latch area of her neck.

I took my mare back to Milliron Clinic after two months. Pete removed the cast. He gave me instructions on how I was to tell Jim Bonnett how to nail the shoe to the mended hoof. With the grace of God, Pete's surgical gifts, and Jim Bonnett's farrier abilities, I've been riding my girl ever since!

I miss Pete and the comfort of knowing that no matter what he could fix my horse's injuries. I think about him often and the times he would come to my barn. I'm so thankful he was always there to help me and my horses. He was truly a gifted man with animals and medicine.

Pat's Snake

Jody Smith

One of Pete's clients was a young minister from an evidently conservative church. When the congregation learned he was a budding herpetologist and was keeping snakes in the manse, he was ordered to remove them. This was difficult since it was winter. He asked Pete's help in rehoming one. Pete brought the large blacksnake to the farmhouse to keep until spring. Our son, Pat, was delighted and agreed to help care for it and its sturdy cage. A small colony of white rats was provided by the client as food for "Pilot." I became fond of the rats and when Pete came down the basement to select the snake's dinner, I was distressed. Pete decided to give the rat an anesthetic and drag the sleeping rat across Pilot's cage. Jessica, our daughter, and I went to the barn and left Pete and Pat to "their chores."

Later in the evening, as I was preparing to get in bed, Pete said, "Better wait a minute, I need to check on Pilot."

"What?" I asked, and then noticed the snake's cage, in our living room, was empty. The anesthetic was correct for the rat, but as the snake absorbed it, he had become too sluggish, so Pete had put him in a pillowcase in our bed with the electric blanket turned up. Needless to say, Pilot was returned to his cage before I entered the bedroom again.

That week I was invited to a meeting of the local women's Chit Chat club in nearby Amesville. As I was regaling them with my recent adventure, they looked at me as if I was from Mars. That was my first and last meeting. I didn't get invited back.

Pat was sad and I was relieved when he and Pete took Pilot out to his new home in the woods when spring came.

Even living for several months in close proximity to a snake never relieved me of my completely illogical fear of non-poisonous snakes. One summer as I was doing laundry, a small snake came out from under the washer. I clambered up on the dryer and screamed for Pete. He came down the stairs and said, "Oh, that's just a house snake" and turned to leave. I thought for a moment, then said, "*Peter Smith*, you get right back down here and take that snake out!!" He laughed heartily and took it out beyond the pond to release it.

Mr. Roosevelt
Martha Hansgen

Pete helped my Mister Roosevelt walk again. I got my first puppy from a free box in front of the Athens Kroger one September afternoon in 1985. He was a black and white English Springer Spaniel. I named him Mister Roosevelt to appease my family for not asking if I could get a puppy and to impress my Dad who had always been a good Roosevelt Democrat. Mister Roosevelt became my walking adventurer companion. We had a lot of hikes and good times together.

When Mister Roosevelt was five, I got a call to come home, that something had happened to Mister, he couldn't use his hind legs. We took Mister out to Pete's and he told us Mister had two ruptured discs in his spine, that he had hurt himself frolicking. Pete operated on Mister and told us he would walk again. When I went to get Mister after the operation, he was very quiet and serious for a dog. I didn't know what to do with him. Pete said Mister just wanted to sit in the grass. I took Mister outside in the grass and thought if he wants to sit in the grass, surely he wants to walk again.

First, Mister recovered his continence and then had some water therapy in the bathtub as well as some pinching of his paws to make his legs jerk. He had some rides in a wagon to try to get him interested in walking around again. It was Christmas when another dog was around that Mister got up on his tiptoes and walked across the room for the first time. Then I was pretty excited that he would walk again.

Mister did get better and we had many more walking adventures together. Every year and a half, he would have a weakening of his nerve-damaged leg. We took him to Pete's for a shot so that we could flex and extend his leg to build strength.

When Mister was twelve, going on thirteen, and winter was turning into spring, Mister had another relapse only worse than before. My dad died, Mister was weak in his back leg, and I began to wonder what I could do with him if he couldn't walk anymore. Once he collapsed in the mud and another time he pooped all over in every room in the house, a long trail of poop. I had Mister put to sleep and it was only sometime later that I asked Pete if Mister could have gotten better. Pete said Mister Roosevelt just wanted to sit by my side. Now I think that would have been nice, to sit in peace beside Mister Roosevelt.

Tasha

Milena Miller

UPON MY RETURN to Athens from California in 1971 to finish my undergrad degree, I learned about a horse whose owner wanted to give her away. I had always wanted a horse but knew next to nothing about them. Tasha was an 18-year old mare who had been a jumper in her day, until a horse trailer accident that psychologically damaged her forever. When I first saw her standing in the field, her ribs were sticking out, flies were swarming around her body, and she seemed in need of rescue. When we arrived on our farm outside of Guysville, it was clear that she needed help and so did I.

My friends suggested there was a new vet in the area who might come to the farm and examine her, and that his name was Abbott Smith, but he was called Pete. And visit our farm he did with his youthful, cowboy swagger and a bag of heavy tools. Tasha needed worming, her hooves were a mess, and she had bots. In one visit, Pete and I became friends. I learned a lot about horses. He taught me how to feed her, clean her hooves, approach her, groom her, bridle her, but never to ride. Pete rode with a Western saddle and she was bred to carry an English rider. She was stubborn and big, but not a match for Pete Smith.

I began to rescue dogs, cats and birds. I became a 'regular' at Pete's. Once in a while, he and his wife would appear at one of my local outdoor concerts with my band. He was opinionated and so was I, and mostly we agreed upon a host of subjects.

In 1977, I returned to California for what I thought would be a temporary stay. I had to make arrangements for my horse Tasha, so I moved her to a farm belonging to my friend, one who was close to Milliron Clinic. From a distance, Pete continued to stay in touch with me about the care of my horse. One day, in the late 1980's, he phoned me in L.A. to say that it was time to give Tash some peace. She was over 30 years old by now and he was afraid she would go down in her stall. My friend was able to walk Tash to the clinic barns, where Pete euthanized her and buried her with his bulldozer in the front field. He never charged me a dime.

When I returned to Athens in 1996 for a master's degree,

one of the first friends I called upon was Pete. I took my dog and cats to meet him, and we reminisced and shared stories about the social and political climate, something we were to do until he died.

During another trip to California in 1999, my dog suffered a severe stroke. Again, Pete was on the phone, telling me the sad news and assuring me he would take care of my dear Jack. He was always honest in his assessment of what extent of care was best and he always knew what I would want to do.

I was on the way to an appointment the night Pete drove his pickup truck into a tree on Route 550, near the church. It would be one year before his death, though at the time, I thought he would be a man of nine lives. When I realized it was him, I returned to the scene to find my roughneck friend badly shaken, yet otherwise seemingly unhurt. I begged him to go to the ER, but he refused, telling me to meet him back at the clinic with my dog. Jody was there and I suggested he might need more care than he imagined which was precisely what occurred later that night. Six months later, he had hip surgery and recovered well. He was finally out of pain, after years of accidents and hobbling around. When I learned about the farm accident that would claim his life, I still thought it was just another mishap from which he would bounce back. I even sent him a photo of his surgery on my dog Alice and told him to get his butt back at work. But this time, after a lifetime of caring and service to thousands of animals and their owners, and years of building up friendships in our community, he would not return.

I sang at his memorial service. I knew he would like that very much. And to this day, despite having seen all the new docs at the clinic and liking them all, I still say, "I have to take Arthur out to Pete's." As the Byrd's sweetly sang in the 1960's, *He was a friend of mine, his killing (death) had no purpose, no reason or rhyme; He was a friend of mine.*

Woozle

Annette Noyes

In the Fall of 1999 I adopted a retired racing Greyhound, Woozle. Woozle, thanks to his training at the track, was perfectly mannered, walked delicately on leash, and *always* came when called. I adored him, and his "sister" Heffalump, a Great Dane who adored him, too.

My father and his wife retired to Athens County on Hooper Ridge Road in August of 2000. I lived in Pittsburgh at the time and often visited with my dogs. Dad had not yet built a dog fence, but there were ample trails through the woods, and the dogs loved the exploration opportunities. Woozle was allowed to walk with us off-leash, but Heffie, not the sharpest knife in the drawer, had to stay on leash at all times. Hindsight tells me I should have kept Woozle on a leash, too.

One fine October morning we were walking through the

woods. Woozle spotted something and took off. I called in my sternest voice that he *always* obeyed, but he didn't obey this time. Once he was out of my sight, I heard the agonized yipe of a wounded animal. I did a cursory search then hustled Heffie back to the house and sounded the alarm for more volunteers. Eventually, I saw Woozle emerge from the woods as I stood across an open field from him. I raced to his side and could see immediately he was a very unhappy camper. Since he was partially white, I could see dark purple bruises forming on his chest and made note of cuts under his eye. I quickly surmised he had been kicked by a deer. From various sources, I understood the signs of neural deficits in a dog. Woozle was exhibiting classic symptoms, and I concluded he probably had a concussion.

Upon returning to the house, both Dad and Beth, my stepmother, suggested I take Woozle "down the hill" to Doc Smith. Literally two miles away. I led Woozle to my small Honda Civic sedan, and he climbed in the back seat. We then drove down the winding, bumpy road to the Milliron Clinic. Woozle hopped out of the car on his own. I explained what I believed to have happened, and Doc Smith immediately ordered a full schedule of X-rays. We put the poor dog onto the X-ray table. We flopped, pressed, and held him in every position possible. He never so much as whimpered.

Once the X-rays were ready, Doc Smith popped them on the light board and said (verbatim, direct quote!), "I'll be damned! This dog has a broken neck! In two places!" My heart sank knowing full well that Woozle would not be coming back home with me. Then Doc Smith cheerfully declared that he would operate immediately and put a plate in to stabilize the dislocation break at C4-C5. Another vertebra between Woozle's shoulder blades had one of its "wings" broken off, but Doc Smith said a) he probably couldn't get to it very easily, and b) it was something that probably didn't require intervention anyway.

While I love all my animals like my own children, I am a responsible pet owner and know when "it's time." While Doc Smith was nattering on and mentally planning the operation, I interrupted him and said that while I was willing to sell my car to cover vet bills, but I wasn't going to prolong my poor Woozle's agony. Doc Smith immediately replied he could SAVE this dog. He wasn't trying to make a pretty penny from a big operation, he wanted to, and believed he could, save Woozle's life. I left Woozle in Doc Smith's care and went home in tears. The next day I picked up a very battered and beleaguered dog. I then took him home to Pittsburgh, and with the help of my local vets, commenced the extensive after-care and recovery Woozle needed. Within a week he was ready to play outdoors in his yard at home; I didn't permit him to do more than sun himself for half an hour. Then it was back to his crate for full bed-rest.

Woozle was seven at the time of his unfortunate mishap. He lived another seven happy, healthy years and finally died of old age just weeks after Heffie. And herein lies another, short, story.

Doc Smith himself aged, his back got stiffer and stiffer. Heffie and Woozle were much too big to be up on his exam tables. When they came in for bloodwork every three months (at their advanced ages, I wanted to keep on top of anything that might have been developing), my husband and I would hold our ancient dogs on their hindlegs so that Doc Smith did not have to bend over to get a blood sample from a foreleg vein. One day in August, I knew it was Heffie's time. I called the clinic and explained the situation. I knew Doc Smith no longer did house calls, but maybe just once more he would, so I didn't have to cart Heffie down the rough road during her last moments. The kind receptionist put me on hold, and returned seconds later. She said they still had a few patients in the clinic, but once they closed, Doc Smith would come. Heffie was lying in one of her huge beds in the kitchen with me curled around her. Doc Smith came in; suffered his own aching back to kneel down beside my sweet Heffie, and send her on her way.

Six months later, Doc Smith was also gone. Words cannot express the sense of gratitude and admiration I have for Doc Smith. He was a quirky fellow, but at the same time a brilliant vet and true humanitarian. I miss him dreadfully.

Mitzi
Margaret Patton

Dr. Smith had been my vet for many years and he was the best veterinarian. I had a dog that I had rescued from the dog shelter. Her name was Mitzi. She had problems with her back legs. Dr. Smith examined her and said that she would need surgery. He intended to shave down the femur bone in order to ease her suffering. When he did the surgery, he discovered that she had dysplasia and the bones were very fragile. The femur bone had broken off in his attempt to shave it down. But Dr. Smith was ingenious. He actually devised what he called a "steel basket" that he somehow used to fix the problem. I don't think any other vet could have devised such a miracle to solve the problem. It worked! I was not aware that he had performed such a miracle until sometime later when Mitzi was back in his office and walking normally. Dr. Smith took one look at Mitzi and exclaimed "Praise the Lord!"

The day I got Mitzi from the dog shelter, the man told me that he was going to euthanize all the dogs the next day so that he could clean the kennels! The next day, I went back to the dog shelter and all the dogs were gone. He was telling the truth!

Mitzi was a mixed breed dog who loved the outdoors and hunting. I got her for my aunt and uncle who were in their 80's and lived on a farm. They always had dogs that looked like Mitzi; however, when I took Mitzi to their farm, they decided they didn't want her. It took me a long time to get attached to Mitzi because I picked her out based on what I thought my aunt and uncle would like.

At that time, I was not a customer of Dr. Smith. I realized that Mitzi was having difficulty with her back legs and so I doctored with someone else who completely misdiagnosed her problem. When I took her to Dr. Smith to get a second opinion, he felt her back legs and immediately knew she had a torn ligament. Mitzi had surgery to repair her torn ligament. Some time passed and Mitzi was still in pain. That was when Dr. Smith suggested he could shave down the femur bone to give her more comfort. He created a "steel basket" to help Mitzi get around. I am not sure how the steel basket was designed or how it worked. She was such a good dog and grateful for the care she received. Dr. Smith loved her and appreciated what a great dog she was and that in turn helped me to appreciate what a loyal, sweet dog she was.

I brought Mitzi home and I allowed her to be on my bed (I had to pick her up and put her there, she was unable to jump up). I may have caused the next part of the surgery problem - Mitzi was in really bad pain, so I took her back to Dr. Smith. Somehow the steel basket had gotten bent. I suspect I may have caused it as she may have tried to jump down off the bed, I'm not sure. Dr. Smith had to do a second surgery on Mitzi because of the bent basket. When I went into the clinic to pick her up, I just pulled out my credit card, ready to pay for the second surgery, but Dr. Smith said, "*No charge.*" You don't hear that around many vet's offices.

When Mitzi fully recovered and Dr. Smith saw her walking with ease, he said, "Praise the Lord." That's how I know that he had done something miraculous for Mitzi.

Later, Mitzi got cancer and we had to put her down. Even when she was in great pain her tail wagged when she saw Dr. Smith.

Toxoplasmosis
Tom Reid

Our dog started running a fever. She became listless and very hot one evening. It was well after normal office hours, but I called Milliron Clinic anyway. Pete returned my call a few minutes later, having listened to my message, and told me to bring the dog into the office. He was immediately concerned by her symptoms and had me help him hold her down so he could draw arterial blood (although by this time she didn't have much fight left in her). He took the sample a few steps away to a microscope where he spent five or ten minutes studying the sample. He diagnosed that my dog had become septic, infected in her bloodstream with both gram-negative and gram-positive bacteria. He said she likely wouldn't have survived the night. He hooked her up to an IV to push a blend of antibiotics and a lot of fluids. A couple of hours later he sent me home with antibiotics to administer. Due to his expertise as a vet, his skill as a pathologist and his compassion as a good person he saved my dog.

On a lighter note, I brought a cat in for a blood draw to check for toxoplasmosis because we just found out we were expecting a child. Pete asked me to bring the cat back to the operating area because we were going to need to bag her and asked that I assist him. As I came back, Pete was cleaning up the operating table. He was about to sweep six little tails that he had just cropped from a litter of puppies. He looked at me, paused for a second with that sparkle in his eyes, and said "Shame to waste them – maybe we should just make a stir fry." Took me a minute to crack up and he appreciated that I got his humor.

I greatly enjoyed knowing Pete and still miss him. I'm glad that they've kept Milliron operating. The new vets, supported by the original staff, are doing a great job.

Cody
Dorothy Pugh

I think it was 1989, but I'm not real sure of the year. We went on a horseback riding trip to Middle Mountain, West Virginia, a primitive campground. Riders included Nancy Huffman, Dave and Vicki Williams, Pete, Jessica (Pete's daughter), Rich (Jessica's husband), Jim Hoon, Eric and Rhonda Curfman, and myself. We all became good friends.

We rode every day; had a great time. My mule Cody was hard to hold back. One day, we rode the road for approximately two miles and approached two trails – one to the right, one to the left. Everyone was bunched up, stopped, deciding which trail to take. I let Cody decide, and he started on the left-hand trail at a fast walk. I relaxed the reins and really enjoyed my ride. I could hear horses behind me and supposed the whole bunch was there. When I got to the main road, I found out a couple was behind me, they were going on a short ride. I rode for a couple more miles, or so, then decided I needed to turn back the way I came before I was really lost. As I came up on the main road, there was a rider reading the forest marker sign. It was Pete. He was lost, too.

Pete and I traveled back up the road, finally taking a trail trying to find the rest of the crew. Away we went. We almost got stuck in bogs; crossed creeks, climbed mountains, getting off once to lead the horses through unsafe trails. Jessica had Pete's lunch in her saddlebags. Finally, we stopped to rest a few minutes. I shared my lunch and water with Pete.

Long last, we found tracks and followed them, knowing we would come back to camp. I told Pete, "You know what. We are going to be in for." Pete said, "I know."

I told Pete, "When we ride into camp, let's hold hands and call each other *Honey*." He said, "Okay." And so, we did.

Everyone had a good laugh out of it. It's a great memory of a wonderful day with Pete that I'll never forget. This is what is so wonderful about camping; having our wonderful animals, making great memories with wonderful friends.

Hound Dog

Bruce Ruessman

In 2009, we purchased a Bloodhound puppy. We took her to Milliron Clinic for her first vet visit. After checking in with Karen, the receptionist, we sat in the waiting area with other pet owners. The clinic was a hub of activity, with people coming in and out of the clinic, bringing and picking up pets.

Finally, it was our turn, and the vet assistant took us to an examination room. When Pete came in and took a look at her, he started singing *You Ain't Nothin' But a Hound Dog*! We all had a good laugh.

In September 2009, the puppy needed a hip operation. She did very well through the surgery and recovered completely. After the operation, Pete gave us pictures of the whole operation.

"Hound Dog" in surgery

Milk Jug Mare

Marcia Adams

Pete Smith is a name that will forever be etched in my memory. Not a day goes by without the mention of his name when someone talks about their animals. He was by far the best veterinarian I have ever met and trusted.

Pete was not only good with small animals (ten pounds or under), but with animals a thousand pounds plus. I was always fascinated when I would watch how he handled these majestic massive animals...I am speaking of horses.

I had the honor of meeting Pete in the mid 1980's when I chose to board my horses with Jimmy and Nancy Bonnett in West Virginia. I remember Nancy talking about how good he was with animals. My first encounter with Pete was when he came to the Bonnett's barn to float all the horses' teeth. I thought at first that he was a boarder like myself and asked him which horse belonged to him. He chuckled and told me he was the vet. I was so impressed because he was so "down to earth" and not the least bit pretentious. He was a well-educated man who never "talked down" to you, but used laymen's terms that anyone could understand.

I bought a beautiful black pacer mare in the late 1980's. The Bonnetts told me to make sure she had been vaccinated against strangles (the disease that they feared was running through the barn and could be fatal). I was told she had been, but unfortunately I was misinformed. My mare, that I had only had a few weeks, contracted the disease.

It was a Saturday morning when the Bonnetts contacted me about the situation with my mare. I immediately drove to the barn to find my horse with very labored breathing. Nancy managed to get an oxygen tank and I stood in her front yard with a hose in my horse's nose to help her breathe. Nancy called Pete who had to drive from Athens, Ohio (at least one and a half hours away). I will never forget standing in Nancy's yard with this beautiful mare that I had just purchased, thinking she was going to die and how much money I was going to have to spend for a vet bill.

Pete arrived that afternoon, spoke to me and began looking at my mare. He then asked Nancy if she had an empty milk jug. I seriously wondered where he was going with this. He looked at me and told me to hold my mare as still as I possibly could. Pete then proceeded to cut the handle off the milk jug and made a slit in my horse's throat. He put the handle of the milk jug in the hole he had just cut to her throat. Immediately, my mare began to relax and breathe. It truly was a miracle to me. He told me to use peroxide daily and take the milk jug handle out in a week. Two weeks later, I was riding my mare once again. I really thought it was going to be extremely expensive and was totally shocked when he looked at me, laughed and said I owed him $65.00. That, by the way, covered everything. He was definitely in the business to help animals, not make money.

My other fond memories were the wonderful trail rides he had annually every October. He would invite his clients to spend the day riding on his property. Everyone would bring a covered dish and meet at his cabin where some who did not participate in the ride got everything ready for the riders. He had all of the trails thoroughly marked for the expert, intermediate and novice riders. It was a time I will always remember.

I had a Tennessee Walker for almost twenty years. He became ill and guess who I called??? Pete came to the barn and told me it would be best to put him down. The Bonnetts drove my horse and me to Athens, Ohio, the next Saturday morning.

Pete let me spend some time with my horse alone, then we went to lunch. Pete paid for everyone's meal! I chose not to be around when he put my horse down and asked if he would wait until we left to return to West Virginia before he began the process. He buried my Tennessee Walker (Mac) on his property. Once again, I thought it would be very expensive. He charged me $100.00.

Pal-cat

Stephanie Wilson

Words can't express how highly I thought of Pete Smith. He was an amazing and caring vet who is sadly missed. My first experience with Pete was over eighteen years ago when my six-month old female boxer got hit by a car. It shattered her hip and broke her leg. I took her to several animal clinics in Athens that wanted to take her leg off; they said there was no way around it, it had to be done! I wanted her to be fixed back to normal. She was like my child. My last shred of hope was taking her to Pete Smith. I explained the situation and he said, "Bring her out to see me. I can fix her up!" And that is exactly what he did. He put a plate and several pins in her leg. She was as good as new! She had a very happy healthy eleven years with us.

My last experience with Pete was a stray kitten that ended

up having several surgeries over a period of time. This kitten always found ways to find itself on Pete's operating table. The first time Pal-cat got his leg caught in a trap and he had to have a hip replacement. The second surgery he again got the same leg caught in a trap. This surgery was a little more difficult. Pete came out to tell me how Pal-cat was dong and he explained that Pal-cat had to be brought back; that the cat had stopped breathing on the table! Pal-cat fully recovered. The third surgery Pal-cat got his tail caught yet again in something. This time when Pete was done operating he brought out pictures of Pal-cat on the operating table with his little oxygen mask on. Pete wanted to show me what my little guy looked like during his multiple surgeries. Pal-cat is still happy and healthy, now ten years old, with a few extra plates and no tail.

Reuben
Darci Roberts

As many of us know, Dr. Pete was a miracle worker and a person the likes of whom I will probably never meet again. He saved my doggie's leg, and presumably, his life. Some people have the idea, *Oh, it's just a dog*! but Reuben has been far better to me and far more meaningful than half the people I've had the pleasure, or displeasure, to meet. Dr. Pete is certainly the reason for meeting the best friend I've ever had.

I met Reuben, a golden Great Dane, in April 2006. I adopted him when he was five months old. The Amish were going to kill him and I said, "No!" Pete told me to call a local rescue group who offered counseling and financial support.

Due to his mistreatment, Reuben and I became special friends. Reuben needed two surgeries on his foot. Pete said, "The hand of the Lord guided my hands because there was nothing in the foot to work with."

The first surgery went well; the second surgery is when I met Carol Lambert, who was working with a local rescue group at the time. I was sitting outside Milliron Clinic with Reuben. His leg was hanging from where the pin from the first surgery had not held, when Carol pulled into the clinic parking lot. She helped me to locate Pete.

Pete had finished surgery and was ending his day. The minute he saw Reuben he knew what had happened. Bless his heart; another major surgery. Pete never batted an eye. The cast was cut off, he unwound the pile of gauze, placed kind, capable hands on Reuben, and the surgery began. I'll never forget it.

Today, Reuben is fine. His job is to meet the school bus to welcome children home from school. He is a big boy with four strong legs who runs like the wind. Pete did great!

Don't Worry

Horace Karr

There is a small farm pond close to where I live. We had an Irish setter dog that came up missing for a couple of days. My wife had been searching for her and found her caught in a steel trap that had been set to catch muskrats. My wife took the trap off and took the dog to Pete. She told him what had happened and that when she took the trap off the dog, the dog had started to bleed. Pete then said to her, "Then did you put the trap back on?"

I had an appointment to bring one of my horses to Pete's clinic to be operated on. I was on time but no one was at the clinic. I went to the house to let him know I was there. A young boy by the name of Pat answered the door. I told him to tell Pete I was there with the horse, but not to worry, I would wait. The young lad replied, "I will tell him, but he won't worry!"

Sam's Gym

Sam Jones

Pete was a wonderful man and true friend. I met Pete Smith as a veterinarian some thirty-five years ago. He was one of the best when it came to animals. He would go out of his way to help anyone, anytime. He was a man of great courage.

Pete was interested in many things, including boxing and self-defense. He came to my gym after working all day and trained for two or three hours. He would box with professional boxers and enjoy being a sparring partner for them when they were training for a boxing match. If he received a bloody nose or some other injury, he would just laugh about it. Most people wouldn't begin to have the courage to do this. The pro boxers were amazed at this spirit and will to win, knowing he was being defeated. He always gave 100 percent until the bell rang. This is the way he lived his life. When he was involved in a project, he always gave it his all. All the students were always happy to see him. He is truly missed by the boxing family at Sam's Gym.

Flipping Cows

Will Tevis

One time I was on a farm call with Dr. Smith. A farmer had a cow tied up to a railing. The cow was dying; she was in duress. By the time the farmer brought the cow into the barn and waited for Pete, he knew the cow was in trouble; he knows all that. Pete had seen all this before. Quicker than I could imagine and in a manner I don't have a clue, Pete flipped the cow over on her back, front feet tied together. Her back feet fastened similarly, exposing her belly. Do you know anyone who can stand beside a 2,000-pound cow and flip it upside down, then tie its feet up in the air, in less than three minutes? Pete had directed me to find a burlap sack, which I did, and was standing there holding the bag watching him secure the cow. It was then that the magic happened. He pulled out a razor and made a precise cut from her udder to her sternum, reached inside, found her womb, slashed it open, then ordered me to help him pull a calf from her recently opened belly. I did this. These were new sounds, smells, and visuals for me. After the calf fell lifeless to the floor, Pete had me rub it roughly with the burlap sack. I didn't understand the direction exactly, but made an attempt. Pete started sewing and pulling bleeding veins, to make the ends ragged so they could clot better. I was rubbing the calf, no results. Pete broke away, took the burlap from me and started rubbing the calf roughly – Big Pete style of roughly. Almost immediately, the calf came to life. Pete then went back and continued to work on the cow. I bet the whole thing took twenty minutes.

After he sewed the cow up, he cut her loose, made her get on her feet and the roughed-up calf started nursing. There's a lot of things that you have to assume that Pete knows about, that a personality has; it takes a certain type of inner strength to do that kind of stuff. Pete was particularly good with his hands. With tearing those things out of the cow; it's not like a surgeon now, who has something prepped and laying on a table. There wasn't anything in the barn to prepare for this type of birth. It's more than diagnosing what the problem is and directing somebody else to do it, or doing it with a team. It was some guy...me...who just happened to be there at the time. But it wasn't me. It was Pete. He was really good with his hands.

And it wasn't like he was panicking. He was talking and cussing the whole time, but he wasn't upset - he was more irritated with me for not being able to rub the calf.

Fluffy

Jane Richter

Pete held such a special place in our affections. His veterinary practice had long been such an important and special asset to us as well as to the surrounding Athens area. My husband and I arrived in Athens in 1964, still newly married and still without children or pets. It was not until many years later, in the late 1970s, when our young children were in the lower grades that we acquired a pet and had our first encounter with Pete. A friend had found a small dog, matted and hungry, roaming in the woods. She wasn't interested in a pet at the time, but she was sure the Richters would give the dog a good home. We realized we needed help and guidance from a veterinarian. It was our good fortune that a friend recommended Pete Smith. When he saw our sorry looking little dog, he laughed and as he looked her over, he assured us she was a pure-bred cocker spaniel, older, but in good shape generally, and that she would look much better if we had her groomed. She did. Our children, Steve and Katie named her Fluffy and together we visited Pete many times during her life. We were delighted to have found such a top-notch vet with a wonderful sense of humor who seemed to like kids as well as animals. We were never disappointed.

As Pete had cautioned us, Fluffy was not a young dog. Eventually she lost her sight, first in one eye and then the other. Pete told us that she didn't need her sight as much as we humans needed ours, and she would be fine. We relocated furniture to make it easier for her to navigate in the house, and there it stayed. She still enjoyed her walks outdoors on her leash. Over time her sightless eyes became infected and had to be removed. Again, Pete assured us she was good for more years, and since she was already blind, the removal of her eyes would not be an extra trauma. And he suggested that if we let the curly hair on her head grow just a bit, no one would notice that she had no eyes. He was right. But in spite of Pete's assurances, the first night we brought her home after surgery, we were up all night worrying. She made strange noises and seemed so uncomfortable. Come morning, Fluffy awakened in bright spirits, happy to be home and eager to continue business as usual while we were the wrecks from our all-night so-journ. She was still the same Fluffy and continued for a few more years to enjoy life and her outdoor walks.

Later when she became ill, Pete diagnosed kidney failure and told us it was time to let her go. She died in my arms as Pete administered her last shot. I took her home and buried her in the back garden. Her death left a void in our household. Shortly, a card arrived in the mail from Pete which contained a poem, "*The Death of a Pet*" written by a professor in the English department. It was such a comforting gesture. He knew how bereft we were, that Fluffy was more than just a dog. She was part of our family. But, until that moment, we had never thought of sending a sympathy card for the loss of a pet. From that time on, we adopted the practice.

We had more pets and Pete was right there with us, helping us give them a good and healthy life. First was "Kitty," a gray and multi-tabby, who found us and moved in. Then Thena, a small sheltie, who came temporarily while her "family" spent the year in England. They, however, decided to make England their home and we happily adopted Thena.

When our daughter, Katie, was between ten and twelve she decided she just might want to be a veterinarian. It was during those years that the British program, "*All Creatures Great and Small*," was aired on American TV, and our family watched every episode together. That program coupled with our many visits to Pete's certainly influenced our daughter's decision. Being animal lovers ourselves, we were immensely pleased and suggested she talk to Pete during our next visit. She did ask an intelligent question or two and then wondered how many vacations and days off he had each year. He paused, looked into the distance as if to be thinking, rubbed his chin, and said "I believe I had a day off back in 1963." He actually gave a specific day which I no longer remember. It was quite funny but I believe he was letting her know the realities of being a veterinarian. Katie has always remained an animal lover and volunteered in shelters and various animal programs, but, alas, she did not choose to become a D.V.M.

I developed allergies to animals and after our last pet died, grief stricken though we were, I knew it would be unwise to get another. I love animals, but the pet-free house improved my health and my breathing immeasurably. It was the end of an era for us, no more pets and no more visits to our vet. Still it was comforting to know that Pete was still on the job helping others take care of their pets and farm animals. And suddenly he wasn't. That truly was the end of an era.

Mailman
Dale Saylor

My first contact with Dr. Pete Smith was when he first came to Athens County and worked at the Athens Veterinarian Clinic in 1963-1964. We lived in New Marshfield on a small farm with a few animals. I had a sick cow and he came and treated it. It was during cold weather. Jody and their young children came with him. He kept the pickup truck running and the heater on for them.

In 1978 I transferred to Athens as a rural carrier and started delivering the mail for the Milliron Clinic. I was also Pete's personal mailman. During the next seventeen years, I grew to know Pete, Jody, Jessica, and Pat really well. There were times I would see Pete at the mailbox, or if I had to deliver something over to the clinic that had to be signed for, one of us would say something for a good laugh. After Pete's first grandson was born, I said, "How is the new grandson?" and he said, "He is an exceptional child."

Another time he pulled up behind me at the mailbox and came up to the car to get the mail. One of the young boys was with him and as Pete walked up to the car, the small boy climbed out of the window and on top of the car. Pete told him to get back in the car and looked at me and said, "That kid needs his ass busted." I'm sure grandpa never did that.

Later we had a young heifer that was trying to deliver a calf that was too big and we tried to get a local vet, but they were all too busy with their patients. We were able to get a vet from Logan who took the calf and saved the heifer. Later, after hours at the clinic, Pete came out after dark to check on the cow. I appreciated that.

Peyton
Debbie Sheskey

On September 15, 2012, Peyton, our sixteen-year-old cat, and I are headed across Route 550 to Milliron Clinic. It is a beautiful, golden September day in southeastern Ohio. It seems as if all should be right with the world, but Peyton had a seizure and has stopped eating. He has had a good, long life but I am hoping he can get better. Thinking of the many times Peyton and I have made this trip and the many conversations Dr. Smith and I had about his care, it doesn't seem possible that Pete won't be on the other side of the bridge when we arrive at the clinic.

My dad and I rescued Peyton from the weeds along a neighborhood road, Trash Pile Road, when he was just three weeks old. He was tiny but mighty. He ate the cat litter and

Dr. Smith told us that Peyton was too young to know the difference between cat litter and cat food. Peyton once had a tumor which Dr. Smith removed. Traumatic for all; but thankfully it was not malignant. One Christmas Eve he hid in the closet and came out limping. Dr. Smith helped us the day after Christmas. It was an abscess and with treatment Peyton recovered quickly. Dr. Smith was always there when Peyton needed help and we miss him.

We roll over the familiar sound of the cattle bars, across the bridge and into the parking lot. We are greeted with the same enthusiasm and respect as always. Karen has worked us into the appointment schedule. Dr. Galvin asks me to explain exactly what happened, how Peyton acted during the seizure, and what has happened since. He recommends fluids and a B12 shot. I leave Peyton under Nanette and Dr. Galvin's care for a few hours. When I return I am told Peyton is doing okay even though it can and probably will happen again. Peyton and I, armed with more fluids and grateful hearts, head to the car and meet Jody on the way out. I tell her about Peyton and she is so kind, telling me that Peyton couldn't have a better owner. The sun is shining still this September afternoon and Peyton and I head home. As we cross the cattle bars, we feel Pete is smiling on all of us. I have taken many pets, mostly rescues, to Milliron Clinic for over forty years. Dr. Smith taught everyone to respect and care for animals. His life was rich with many admirable accomplishments, but to me this is his greatest legacy.

Kane

Carol Lambert

In August 1982, my family and I moved to Athens from Fort Wayne, Indiana, to be part of the local Radio Station WATH. On the third day in town I realized that my Husky had an abscess and needed help. I called a neighbor for information on who to call. She suggested a vet in The Plains or Milliron Clinic.

I called the vet in The Plains (we were renting a house in The Plains) and the vet could not see my Husky for several days. I called Milliron, a Dr. Smith picked up the phone. I told him my concern. He said, "I am going into surgery but I'll wait for you." He gave me directions to Milliron Clinic. That was over thirty years ago. Dr. Smith became my vet and close friend.

Several years ago, I told Dr. Smith that Bob, my husband,

and I were having a difficult time finding land on which to build. Dr. Smith thought he could help, stopping everything and driving me down State Route 550. The rest is history, because of his faith in the Lamberts, Bob and I created Deerview Acres.

Because of my interest in dog rescue, Dr. Smith became "Pete" as he worked with me and several hundred dogs. Many office visits were routine, however, during a number (my dogs and rescue dogs) of visits magic happened in surgery. Some surgeries Pete had nothing to work with, commenting later on the hand of the Lord was guiding his hands.

So many dogs were under Dr. Smith's care from my direction. Kane was a male dog, maybe five years old, an American Pit Bull, who came from a very rural area close to Athens; an area where Pit Bulls were used for dog fighting or just killed. Kane was taken in as a stray by a kind lady. She must have had lots of glass around the floors in her home, because an accident happened and Kane's hind leg was badly severed – he was bleeding to death. A friend took him to a vet, but the vet refused to help. The dog owner put a tourniquet on Kane and called me. I told her to drive to Milliron Clinic and Pete would help. I called ahead; Pete was waiting and managed to put a severed leg back together. He really liked Kane.

Kane lives with me now. He has four strong legs. He is my

buddy and a friend to all the other rescues who live at my home.

Pete never turned one of my rescue dogs away. I did not know until later that many vets (up to this time) would not help Pit Bulls. Pete always helped whatever animal needed help – even my geese.

Dr. Smith took care of so many animals and their owners for so long. I am grateful to have had Pete for a friend and vet. He will always be part of me.

Rowdy
Amber Moore

I met Dr. Smith when I was eighteen with my first dog, Rowdy. I went to him from there on out, and recommended him to many others throughout the years. I could offer a lot of memories from over the years, but I will try to be short and offer just a few.

I had been taking Rowdy to Dr. Smith on a regular basis for a couple years. He always remembered Rowdy's name but struggled with mine. He offered me an apology for this one day, and I remarked that he didn't need to apologize or remember my name, that he was not my doctor. Pete laughed and remembered my name from that day forward.

Dr. Smith would never turn an animal away that I know of. I had an elderly woman come to me in the middle of the night when her black lab was hit by a car. He had internal bleeding and all I could do to help was drive her to the emergency vet in Columbus. They wanted $300.00 just for bring him in the door. She didn't have that kind of money so we were forced to leave. It was the wee hours of the morning when we made it back. I called Dr. Smith who of course told me to bring him in immediately. By the time we arrived at the clinic the lab was unresponsive and his breathing was very shallow. Pete took him in. Within three hours he had saved her dog, and he made a full recovery in the end. In addition, he didn't bankrupt the lady, and allowed her to make payments. That dog was her whole world, so not only did he save the lab but her as well. He was truly a remarkable irreplaceable man.

Starbucks
Rick Anderson

For ten years Pete took care of my two big dogs, a big black mutt Sujo and German shepherd Lucky, and four cats, Snowball, Snowflake, Abe, and Babe. Every time for me it was like going to a Starbucks and having a philosophical and emotional conversation! I don't know how it was for the animals, but they liked Pete.

When I had to put Lucky down and was very upset, Pete and I had a serious talk. Or rather, Pete talked to me, dispensing consolation and philosophy. He said, "We humans must take care of our pets and all the animals. They don't know about death, at least not until the very end. Deer are not aware of what we humans call 'carrying capacity.' They just live. If hunters don't shoot them, they'll starve."

So, I left Lucky with Pete. I was too upset to be a witness.

Afterwards I spread Lucky's ashes on my field. I live over the hill from Milliron Clinic. I walk many times on Pete's peaceful trails, and I know I meet him there!

A poem for Pete by Rick Anderson…

dusk
falling
snow
sky-sown
wind sighs
on these worn Ohio hills

black trunks sway and reach
white earth curves to gray sky
heavy and low
wind moans oh! so old, so unknown
wild white sighs into silent timelessness

full soft flow

wind sighs
for time out of mind
grown old
these snow-covered hills
groan to sky
before ever
be forever

alone
eerily aware
linked to so long ago
somewhen
I walk there
and there

Dog Turd Award
Ted and Katharine Foster

When I was in hot pursuit of my Cavalier King Charles Spaniel becoming the first of his breed to gain the CDX, UD, and TD, Pete started (and continued) to give me a hard time about possibly winning the "Dog Turd Award" (Dog folks will recognize the Award Pete meant!). We never did win that award. Years later, Pete consoled me as I wept at the loss of another special Cavalier. And years after that, Pete supported me in my journey to ordination as an Episcopal priest. What a joy and privilege it has been in these later years to preside at Communion Services that Pete was attending.

If you really wanted to get Pete's goat when you took your dog to Pete, all you had to do was say, "My puppykins needs his anal glands emptied." After much rolling up of sleeves and grabbing of cotton, Pete would do the deed, but not happily!

Career Education

Joan Linscott

Pete was an interesting character. A long time ago career education was a big deal in education. The idea was to familiarize teachers with other professions. As a teacher, you were allowed to take a day and go observe someone, and I choose Pete. He was my vet and I knew him. I knew he did surgeries on horses; I own horses and I am a huge horse fan. I went to see him at Milliron Clinic.

Pete had a facility next to his regular office which I had never been in. The facility had a hydraulic surgery table. The horse he was vetting that day was owned by Amish people and they were there, which added to drama to the whole thing. There was a huge horse being prepped to go on the surgery table. I watched as Pete stepped to the operating table. Pete

72

and his staff were putting a horse on the vertical hydraulic table. Obviously, the horse had some kind of calming, because I couldn't believe how compliant it was. As they put the horse up to the table and as they put the horse under, the horse starts to fall. The table comes right up under the horse. I just couldn't believe the whole thing! I hadn't seen anything like it! The horse was huge! Pete was into the horse all the way up to his shoulder. I never experienced anything like that in my life. It was quite interesting. The horse came back and gained consciousness. The surgery over, they reversed the action of the table.

I never interacted with Pete during the surgery, I was just an observer. I looked through the glass into the surgery room, watched as Pete dealt with the Amish people and talked with them about the surgery.

I think the cool thing about Pete Smith is he was doing major, major surgeries. I thought he was an excellent doctor. Not to mention, as I became a member of the community, I realized that he was, too, and that he owned property in Ames Township. Pete was personable, very thorough, and made you feel very comfortable with what he was doing. I had never known a vet like him. He was one of those people who had such a character about him; that curly hair and great personality.

Peanuts Christmas

Anna Lucas

Dr. Abbott Pliny Smith, Pete Smith, was someone who I am grateful to have met in my lifetime. Milliron Clinic was a place that I always felt welcome. Dr. Smith was an interesting man, especially when it came to his work with animals, and how he came to love what he did, every day. Jody, his wife, and Pete had a great farm, which was just up the hill from his veterinary clinic.

I worked for Pete for three years, but I learned so much in those years. When I refer to the kind of person that Pete was in terms of veterinary medicine, "multi-talented" is what I always say. Because we were able to do on the spot emergency cases that sometimes would lead to an equine stomach twist - colic surgery, or to a canine ACL repair.

Before any type of surgery, he would always sit down with

his many books and intensely study the procedure he was going to perform. We would ask him what music he would like to listen to, and it would always be classic, or backyard swing band. In 2009, I bought him the *Peanuts Christmas* CD for Christmas. Somehow it played in the CD player every so often until July.

Pete was amazing at diagnosing equine illness. Clients would travel from southern Ohio and West Virginia for his expertise. Through rain or snow we were at the horse barn by 7 a.m. cleaning stalls, giving medications, and making sure his morning cocoa was ready (Pete's cocoa was a secret recipe). The smaller animals in the clinic were usually there, too, waiting for simple surgeries or appointments.

Around 7:45 to 8:00 a.m. we would hear his dually-diesel truck pull in and his big white truck door slam. Pete was ready to work and looked very sharp. After his work was done in the evening, he would go and swim for an hour at Ohio University before he went home. He was always in shape and ready to go.

When I first met him, he gave me a lot of tips. One that I will never forget is "If you haven't worked a 14-hour day, your work probably isn't done." My work ethic now is a lot like this. He taught me about being thorough and checking my work.

A great memory involves a horse twitch and Pete's nose. During an appointment out in the barn, I *thought* I had a rowdy horse's nose twitched for all of our safety. Pete and I were ready to float the horse's teeth. I was holding the nose twitch so hard and the chain wasn't all the way locked when it slipped off and knocked Pete smack in the nose! After many yelled words, I saw blood on the ground and it wasn't coming from the horse...my reaction was to just start crying. I felt horrible, but it ended up a joke, and I didn't lose my job!

Pete's laugh was contagious and very loud, but enjoyable. His love for animals radiated out into the community, surrounding cities, and states. We would always get the emergency phone call and Pete would say, "Yea, bring it in, we will take a look at it." The next question from the client usually was "How much will it cost?" If they couldn't pay for it, he would find a way and that is why he had so many loyal clients. They knew Pete would always be there to help them out.

Dowager
Gladys Stern

When our son was a young teenager (he is now almost fifty years old), our black Labrador at age ten was having several health problems and we (the family) discussed having to put her down knowing she would not last the summer. Our son was an avid reader of super hero comics when he named the dog Thor despite the fact that she was female. He thought of her as some kind of hero and gender was not an issue. However, as she grew into maturity, I called her the Dowager because she always sat at attention while we had dinner, patiently waiting for something to drop to the floor while salivating profusely. Her body posture was so elegant, her eyes fully focused on the eaters, never making any sounds to call attention to her desires. She was innately polite.

We brought her to Abbott who agreed that the dog was

suffering and it would be a kindness to end her life as soon as possible. He gave the injection and the result was immediate. Knowing that my son would be devastated, he suggested that we take the dog home and have my son dig a grave on our property. Many hours later, after digging through hard soil, my son was physically exhausted and emotionally spent. The therapy worked and though we often thought about the dog, we all felt we had done the best we could for her with the wise advice from Abbott.

Furballs

Georganne Thomas

What can we say except Pete was unique. He was highly intellectual, yet common. He was available anytime! Were it not for his expertise in English bulldog health issues and breathing problems we could never have raised our beloved dogs. He delivered (by C-section) several litters with no losses. He even made house calls for shots, etc. I remember one time I passed by his tea or coffee cup and mentioned to him there was an animal hair in it. He said, "I don't worry about one hair. It's the fur balls you have to watch out for." Then laughed that special laugh of his.

Pete touched so many lives. To many of us, our pets are treated as family members, and he knew how much we loved our pets. He showed great compassion during the end of their lives. Memories of Pete will remain with us for our lifetime.

Bubba

David Sturbois

We had a part Rottweiler and part hound that someone dumped at the farm when he was a puppy. My wife Judith named him Bubba. He was devoted to her and would have gladly given his life to protect her. He liked to run deer and one day he came back with his right rear leg loose in the hock joint. This was obviously a serious injury. Off to Milliron Clinic we went. I said to Pete, "I know that my philosophy has always been that if it is more than $100 the animal is probably not worth it and it will not recover anyway. This is the exception." Pete knew he had me here. He said he could operate and regain some function but he could not promise complete recovery. He built a pulley system inside the dog's leg with wire and screws that replaced what I remember to be the ACL. After a six-week period of restricted movement and six more weeks of semi-restriction, Bubba moved as he always had and did so for another six years till the day of his death.

Bubba was at the clinic several times during his lifetime. He always seemed to understand that it was for his own good, even when he was neutered. Later, he was back to the clinic for something else. I received a call from Pete's assistant and she said that Bubba had a problem. There is a word for it; it is the condition where a male has one testicle dropped down, but not the other. Bubba had one testicle at the time. I told the nurse that Pete had castrated him some time ago. She went away to talk to Pete. She returned and informed me that there would not be a charge to complete the job.

One time Pete asked me how Tully was (a female cattle dog that I had had for a while). I told him that her systems were failing and she was in a lot of pain, so I shot her. Pete looked over at Judith and said, "How are your systems Judith?"

Lisa

Roland Swardson

Lisa was a beautiful Samoyed-Spitz who was great with the family but terrible with strangers, especially veterinarians, and more especially after she got to know them. She got to know Pete very well. Pete knew her very well, too, and though this meant knowing a bitch (in the more-than-technical sense) he never showed the least resentment of her hostile behavior toward him. Though never warm with her, he was gentle, understanding and professional. I admired his self-control as, through more and more visits, he put up with her sullen, uncooperative, ill-natured behavior (that's all I mean by *terrible*, she didn't bite or bark).

It was at people out on the bike path that she barked. Meet a dog, fine. Meet a jogger and there's hell to pay. Lisa barking and growling, the poor runner fending her off, and me yelling commands Lisa paid no attention to. So I was hot for a way to get Lisa to pay better attention. Well, Pete showed me a way. We had moved out to a farm for the summer and Lisa had discovered the joy of chasing a neighbor's chickens. She would not attend to our commands to stay. The problem got serious when she killed one of the chickens and the neighbor threatened to shoot her next time she came on his property. We explained the problem to Pete. He suggested we hang a dead chicken around her neck and make her carry it around until she hated the sight of a chicken.

Well, there was the problem of getting ahold of a dead chicken, outside of the neighbor's supply, so I put that off. But the bike-path behavior was immediate. "We seem to have a built-in attention problem with this dog. What can we do?"

"Well," said Pete, looking hard at Lisa," the next time she ignores you and goes after a runner you can do this." And he put one hand on Lisa's hind back, the other on her front back, lifted her up and shook her as if she were a bunch of rags. Her legs were rolling, her neck was waggling, her tongue was hanging out, and everything was going. It went on for some time. "That's what you do," Pete said after he had gotten his breath. "It's effective because it's what dogs do to their small prey. They shake them to death, and it shows mastery. Do it to them and they feel helpless. They'll remember that the next time you give them an order."

Well, it was good professional advice. What he recommended worked pretty well. But what makes this worth telling to people who knew Pete is this question, one that lingers in our minds: "Was that shaking of Lisa a pure, 100% professional demonstration or was there some feeling in it? Was Pete possibly giving way to the emotions I would have felt after dealing with that stubborn, uncooperative beast for two years? I would have been seething, but I was human. Was Pete superhuman?"

I should tell you that I have consulted my wife, Mary Anne, on this question. I think she is unsure, but she did say this about the shaking: "He was certainly giving it his all."

Lisa never did bite anybody, and I would say that. Those things you describe are not amusing - they will horrify your audience. And they are not accurate. We ourselves taught Lisa not to chase joggers on the bike path. And, actually if you want to be accurate, Pete did the shaking to tell us how to keep Lisa from going after Mr. Pidcock's chickens across the street at the farm. Anyhow I would omit paragraphs two, three, four, and five. Then I would say that we consulted him after Lisa had really been bad - killing a neighbor's chicken. Then say that Pete said, "The next time she even looks like she is thinking about a chicken, you..." and go on with the rest of it.

Pete was a special person. We used to have great times with him when he came out to the farm. He would often stay and have a bite with us and would have us laughing at his wonderful stories; how happy he made everybody, even when they were worried. He will be much missed by all. He was also our vet back when we had animals. He would do double duty - coming to the farm and treating the horses, then entertaining us afterwards with his wonderful stories. Thanks for it all, Pete.

Stifles
Jim Greene

I first met Pete about several years ago. Our horse had a couple of infected teeth and Doc Spindler in Marietta, Ohio, recommended Pete. On arriving at the clinic, Pete quickly determined the problem and that same evening removed the infected teeth. Over the next year and a half, we had Pete treat that same mare and another young filly for stifle.

Both Sandy, my wife, and myself were impressed with Pete's capable skill and even more so with his *down home* easy-going style. Once Pete learned that we had a sawmill and cut timber, he showed us around his mill; his homemade diesel fuel production and his state-of-the-art firewood processor. He told us that his relaxing was done in the woods cutting timber.

In talking to one of Pete's professional friends, a vet himself, he told us that Pete had *come up* the hard way, worked through school to get his education and always kept up with the latest things in vet medicine. They don't make folks like him anymore.

Honey and Shamrock
Carol Wasko

Labor Day weekend, 1980, our family moved to Athens, Ohio. Very soon after, friends found a small, frightened kitten on the court house steps very wet from the pouring rain. They rescued him and brought him to us as a 'welcoming gift.' He had fluffy fur in various shades of dark grey and black. He was beautiful, friendly and seemed happy to have found a home with three children and a very giant Irish Wolfhound, Shamrock. We named him Simon. Upon recommendation by a friend, we took Simon to Dr. Pete for a check-up and immunizations. Dr. Pete informed us that he was a she, so we renamed her Honey.

Honey and Shamrock became fast friends during the day as we were all at work and school. Sometimes she would get outside, but usually stayed in the yard and watched the birds and other amusing creatures. One day, she ran into the street and was hit by a car. We took Honey again to Dr. Pete, and with much effort and care he mended her broken leg and put her back together. We were so grateful and overjoyed.

The following summer we built a house in the country. Just before moving, we dipped Shamrock in dog flea solution, and also dipped Honey into it, not realizing how poisonous it was for cats. Moving day came. Honey appeared to be very ill, so back to Dr. Pete's we went. In route my young son said, "I hope there's no room in kitty heaven today." Through IV's, a long hospital stay, many meds, and tender, loving care, Dr. Pete again saved Honey's life.

Honey went on to live a nice, long life. She was one of our favorite pets. We will always remember the medical expertise, excellent knowledge, and genuine love Dr. Pete had for animals. He touched so many lives, endeared so many people and animals, and left the world a better place. We are grateful for the gift of his life.

Eggbert

Missy Whaley

About twenty-two years ago my loving companion Eggbert, my Airedale-wolfhound mix, had been cut. I had nursed him myself, but didn't succeed with not allowing it to get infected. Waking up one morning, his front right leg was a balloon. I called Dr. Smith. He had me bring Eggbert in right away. No one else was working and I helped as Dr. Smith numbed Eggbert, put a tube in, and drained the infection. I felt empowered because I was afraid of needles, pain, etc. Dr. Smith put me to work. This gave me a purpose, which allowed me to be with my pet and not fall apart. I have flashed back to this moment throughout my life when I have needed courage in other areas of my life.

About five years ago Ash, my Great Dane, was hit by a car. Again off hours, Dr. Smith and an assistant cared for him.

While being efficient, he also was able to speak kindly and with compassion. I appreciated his straightforwardness and putting decisions back to me when there were different options, which I believe he has passed down to his daughter, Jessica. I have enjoyed my interactions with Jessica, too. She is articulate, yet she speaks and gestures with an intention of compassion.

Maya

Connie Winters

My memories of Pete are as varied as he was himself. As the fun jokester and the serious doctor Pete became a part of our lives. I first met Pete soon after my husband and I bought our farm and decided to try raising a few beef cattle. We had no idea what we were doing. Pete came to give them shots and after explaining why and what he was about to do he asked how we contained them. We were clueless. But no matter, Pete got a rope from his car and proceeded to lasso each cow rodeo style. I was in awe. There were countless conversations about dogs, cats, and horses where his advice was often to leave it alone and then there was Maya, my first horse, that I waited twenty-eight years to get. She was my childhood dream come true and I had her for twenty-five years.

Pete had long since quit making barn calls, but when

Maya went down at the very top of our pasture, I couldn't call another vet. Pete had seen us through every bump and sickness…and he put aside what he was doing and came on a perfect Fall day. My neighbor drove him up the hill on his four-wheeler and with gentleness for her and Maya, he quietly put her down. It was terrible, but less so because Pete was there. I will always remember Pete fondly and I count myself lucky to have known him.

Little Black

Amy Abercrombie

I don't have any great stories of Pete Smith. The thing is, he and Jody are the storytellers, and to spend an evening with them was immensely entertaining and memorable. I knew Pete by reputation when I first came to Athens because everyone said what a good vet he was, the best, but he was also expensive, and money was always short in those days, so I didn't avail myself of his professional services for my beloved cat, who was very healthy, anyway. When Ed and I were married in the Good Shepherd Church in Athens, I got to know them both and felt a kinship with them, as they were faithful attenders, and also rather high church, as I was.

Once our old pony, Little Black, was not eating well; he would graze, and then deposit little wads of grass in the pasture, not swallowing, and I asked Jody if Pete would come out and check his teeth. She said he didn't make house calls any-more, but if I invited them to dinner, he might bring his tools.

"How about bean enchiladas?" I asked, as that was one of my specialties. She said he liked anything as long as there was sour cream on the menu, and that was something that made enchiladas all the better. They came and we had a marvelous time with their lively presence. And he checked Little Black's mouth, and said, "His back teeth are all gone!" That is why he wasn't able to eat grass in the pasture. After that, we bought horse meal in big bags that didn't require a lot of chewing, and he lived for some time after that.

Another time, Fluffy, my lovely long-haired ginger cat, was quite ill, and I brought him in to Pete, as the other vets didn't seem to help. Pete fixed him right up and I was inspired to write him a thank-you note, as if written by Fluffy (with paw prints), which ended up on his wall, along with others, as I remember. I remember Pete saying how he had tried living in eastern Colorado for a year, and there was "not a drop of rain," so he felt he couldn't stay there. That was of course in his early days.

This is probably too personal, but Jody told me she was a virgin when they married, and I didn't see how that was pos-sible these days. She said she got him a beer, and he was so tired he would give up on her and fall asleep. So that is how she managed to hold off until marriage.

25 Miles Away
Robert Richmond, D.V.M.

Pete and I had a mutual friend, Bud Strouss, D.V.M. Bud was in my graduating class. Every February, we met up at the Ohio Veterinary Medical Association annual meeting in Columbus, and all three of us got together.

We used to have our regional meetings at the Lafayette Hotel in Marietta. One time, we had a meeting here at my farm. We don't drink beer very much, but we had beer in the refrigerator. Pete took a bottle of beer from the frig and there was something in the bottle. It was old beer. He drank it anyway.

Whenever I got into a problem with a horse that I couldn't figure out, I would call Pete. A couple of times I called him about a foundered horse who was having trouble walking. The horse owner had cut down a tree where his horses stood, a black walnut tree. The horse foundered just by standing in the sawdust from the tree. Pete had X-rayed it and said it was in pretty bad shape and that it wouldn't do very well, and it didn't.

Then another time, there was a colt that was born that wasn't made properly. It had a liver that didn't develop properly. The colt didn't make it. I had to prove to the horse owner what was going on, and Pete was helpful there. They always say you're an expert if you're 25 miles away, so I got Pete, who was 25 miles away.

Cammie

Helen Lantz

A friend highly recommended Pete to us when we were looking for a good (great) equine vet. After getting to know Pete, and then Jody, we became great friends. We looked forward to Pete's October 31st (horseback) trail rides. We invited the Smiths up to ride with us at Salt Fork State Park. Going down the trail, Pete would point out all the trees and tell us their names. I thought to myself, *What a fascinating man. What a life he has had!*

He took care of Cammie, our dog, and she loved him until he had to manipulate her back leg. Her knee cap kept going out of place, and he had to see how easy that happened. After that, she wasn't so fond of him. But he did both her knees (surgery), and at thirteen, she is still moving good.

Pete also taught us how to clean a gelding's sheath. I believe the words he used were "grab hold of it and wash gently with warm water." I still do it that way.

Neighbors
Donnie Wirtshafter

It was the Fall of 1970. We were neighbors of Dr. Smith. We took five abandoned cats to Dr. Smith. That's when we first met. He was fresh out of Colorado at the time. He was the hardest working guy I knew. He had a truck that he could take on farm calls. It was refrigerated and he could do surgery right in the field. That was pretty incredible for 1970. He worked his butt off from early in the day to late at night. His staff was amazing, too. He would do all of his appointments, then he would go work the farm. He was always really funny and accepted everybody.

We were pretty much hippies back in the 1970's and Pete was okay with us. Eric Eisenberg, who worked for Pete, was one of my friends. I met Eric in Jamaica. Pete was instrumental in Eric's decision to go to vet school. We became close friends over the years.

I rode horseback once through Pete's amazing woods. He had accumulated all these farms. He kept adding to his original farm by buying all the surrounding farms. He was land poor. He said he couldn't resist buying another farm. I think he had a couple thousand acres at one time, but he suffered financial strains from buying land.

Pete and his partner decided they were going to farm sheep in Ohio. He hired a shepherd to keep the herd. They were western sheep, not eastern sheep. The weather was a problem for the sheep. It didn't take very long for the sheep to get foot rot. That gave up the idea to be able to pasture them because of the foot rot; 6,000 inoculations for foot rot. It was awful. The buzzards came. There were probably 150 buzzards eating sheep carcasses. The buzzards were living off the sheep that were constantly dying. It was a sight. I was starting as an attorney and I was part of the litigation. Because it was a partnership, it was complex; partnerships are difficult to break up, it's kind of like breaking up a marriage. The court records are available to the public. It's quite the story.

I saw Pete perform surgery on a miniature horse. He built special tables for horses. It was like a surgical theater. He had a world class clinic. They brought him Royal horses and the Saudi horses. A small vet just doesn't get that.

Farm Sitting

Jerry and Ellen Izor

We met Pete at the Athens County Fairgrounds. He was the veterinarian for the Fair that year. It was in 1964. We bought two Quarter Horses, Pepsi and 7up, from Fred Merriman. We were looking for a place to board them and Pete said we could board at his farm. When we had free time, we would go horseback riding through Milliron Farm. Those long trail rides over the rolling landscape were beautiful! What a great memory.

We became good friends with the Smith family. When Pete and Jody left the farm for meetings or other events, we watched over Milliron Farm. We would spend long weekends farm sitting and keeping tabs on Jessica and Pat. We were students at Ohio University. We were looking for fun things to do on the weekends. Farm sitting at the Smith's was always a favorite pastime. We would spend holidays together, too.

We have so many incredible memories of Milliron Farm! Pete and Jody gave us, unselfishly, the opportunity to truly enjoy their farm and family. They are Godparents to our children, Christopher and Katrina.

Uncle Pete

Sharon Barrows

When I was in high school, in the late seventies, our family cat, Tiger, had a miserable sore on her belly. We took her to the vet and he gave us medicine but nothing seemed to help her. We made the decision with the help of a friend in my class to take the cat to Dr. Smith. He discovered the problem was no more serious than a really bad case of fleas. Some shots, ointment and care, and within days the sore was healed and the cat was back to ruling her roost, our house. That was the beginning of many pet adventures with Dr. Pete Smith, who grew into "Uncle Pete."

Pete Smith was always dedicated to his patients, which became a blessing to our household because Pete ended up caring for our long line of thirteen dogs and five cats.

I can still remember vividly the first time Pete met Porky,

a boxer-beagle-basset hound mix. Pete came in, looked down at the table where this little six week old pup that weighed less than a pound was sitting, and began to laugh so hard he had to hold himself up by leaning on the table. This may be the reason why Porky didn't always enjoy his trips to Milliron Clinic; he could still remember the laughter. Porky was a rather independent dog and had a love for chocolates. Not good when you're a canine. Porky and I were a close team, all he had to do was look at me funny and I knew he didn't feel well. A strange look and we would take the trip to Pete's. Pete told me that if he wasn't acting normal, then something must be wrong. He would run a blood test and sure enough, his blood level was down. A few shots and vitamins later he was back to his old self.

The memories of a good dog and his vet go on forever. There was the time when my mother bought a box of candies and left it on her desk. We left the house and came back to find Porky carrying the now empty box down the hall to greet me. He looked very sorry as if to say, "I shouldn't have eaten the whole box." We called Pete and he told us to get some food into him and bring him out. He did a blood test and everything was fine. That's something we loved about Pete. You could call him and he would give us good advice.

Porky lived sixteen years with a smile on his muzzle.

When Porky died, on his way out to the clinic, Pete listened to him so he could definitely pronounce him dead. He gave my mother a hug and told her he knew how much she would miss him.

After losing Porky, we asked Pete if he knew of another dog that needed a home. He introduced us to Daisy, a doxie (Dachshund) mix. She had two puppies that Pete knew would find a home but Daisy, being a mother dog and in rather rough shape, he wasn't so sure about. Once we met her, we were her servants. I think Pete had a clue that would happen. As my sister was fond of saying, "Pete gave us to her." She quickly became Queen Daisy. When we brought her back to have her stitches removed after having her fixed, I put a scarf around her collar and over her back like a cape and tied a foil crown on her head. She walked in kind of shy until all the staff and Pete fussed over our queen. She stood up straight, drank it all in and insisted on being clothed the rest of her days. Pete would shake his head as he waited patiently for us to remove her dress, PJ's or coat.

Pete knew Daisy was a mixed breed, we knew she was a mixed breed, but Daisy never caught on. Pete saw Daisy through so many illnesses from worms to glaucoma but we hit a wall when she developed cancer. We tried surgery and chemo but it just didn't work. Uncle Pete had tears in his eyes as he gave her the final shot. That's one of the reasons we loved Pete because we were family and our pets were family to him.

Soon after Daisy came to live with us, fifteen-week-old Buster came to live with us. He was part Collie and maybe black Lab. Daisy became his adopted mother even though she could walk under him. They often visited Pete together. A good mother always went to the doctor with her child and Daisy really liked Pete. Pete became even dearer to us as he cared for Buster's hip dysplasia. When he would take an X-ray, it was a comfort to us to be there with our dog and get to see the results. I was getting pretty good at seeing abnormalities in the X-rays. Buster was a tall dog and weighed over fifty pounds. Pete would let poor old Buster sit on the floor while he gave him his shots. Buster was a loyal gentle dog but he never seemed to warm to Pete. Pete often said he didn't blame Buster, after all he was always poking his doggy suit with needles and sticking thermometers where it wasn't pleasant. Buster didn't really realize how inconvenient and difficult it was for Pete to lean over and give him shots or take blood samples. Pete never complained. He said he understood how painful arthritis was.

Our family was still growing; we now had Daisy, Buster and added Ozzie, a black Lab mix and his sister Harriett. Oh my, we will never know exactly what happened when Ozzie stayed overnight to be fixed. When we picked him up the next day, Pete told us with all seriousness in his voice that if we wanted a free euthanasia he would be glad to put him down. When we refused the offer he told us, "If that dog were a human he would be an outlaw." We made an effort to take Oz to see "Uncle Pete" on Halloween or April Fool's Day. He always offered the free euthanasia, but when Ozzie blew a disc in his back Pete did surgery to try and save him from being paralyzed. The surgery didn't work but Pete was impressed how Oz never seemed to mind being paralyzed. He actually was impressed when he went to trim Oz's nails and he pulled his leg away. "He has a lot more power than I thought he would. You've done an exceptional job with this one," I will never forget Pete's praise. It meant a lot to me. I also remember how when Ozzie started to fail suddenly and how Pete worked on him in the car so as not to cause him anymore stress. Pete thought Oz's kidneys were failing but it turned out to be his liver. When Pete put him down, Oz was resting his head on my lap and Pete once again had that understanding look in his eyes. I think Pete missed Ozzie most of all.

Ozzie's sister Harriett looked more like Collie or Dalmatian mix. She was often seeing Pete for urinary infections but she had the manners her brother lacked. She would often give us a good wrestling match when it came time for shots. Pete often said we wouldn't know what a normal dog was. He didn't hold that against us though. He was surprised the day he came in and found her body in the back room. He stopped and asked, "Isn't that the Barrows' dog?" He knew our dogs by sight, which did not surprise me, but when you stop to think about all the patients he cared for it does leave me feeling a little more like family.

The dog story continued as we adopted the sisters, Princess and Whiskers. Princess, a hyperactive black Lab mix, was a champion wrestler and a real clown. She would scream and cry from the minute we hit the clinic parking lot until we left the lot. I will always hold a soft spot for Pete because when Princess had gone off the deep end and Pete was ready to put her down, he asked us about it, but I was the emotional one. He gave her some vitamin shots and told me if she wasn't better in a day or two, she should be put down. Unfortunately, she didn't respond. After a day of having chemo myself, we took her out to have her put down. Pete came out with the gurney to take her inside and asked if anyone wanted to go with her; my sister and I went in. Princess seemed to know what was about to happen and wrestled with us to the end. Pete knew what my day was like. He put his arm around me. I really needed that hug. Now that I think about it, Princess was the last dog that Pete sent ahead of us.

After we lost Queen Daisy, we asked Pete if he knew of another dog that needed a home. He introduced us to Oliver, a Golden Deceiver, as Pete called him. My guess would be a cocker spaniel mix. He is a real ray of sunshine for us.

The last dog of these dog tails is Dixie. She is a dapple doxie. When we got her, she was almost wild. She had an infection from a surgery from her former life. Pete opened her up and cleaned up the infection. He was a little upset with the former clinic for not telling him if she had been vaccinated or had rabies shots. I think for Pete it was less about the people and more about the animal. It took us six months before Dixie realized she wasn't a dog anymore. I'm not sure how Pete felt about that but he often said he would love to be a dog in our house.

We also took nearly feral cats to Pete to have them fixed. We warned them about their wild nature. The Mama cat and her sons, Midnight and George, were perfect little cats, but her daughter, Blue, now there's a different story. She escaped from her cage and hid in the wall. We got a call telling us we could pick up the three cats but that they would have to trap the fourth cat and would have to fix her ear. We told them that she loved fish. Some salmon in a live trap did the trick. There's nothing normal about our pets. They needed an extraordinary vet and that we found in Pete.

Pete was a brilliant diagnostician, exceptional vet and a great storyteller. Pete had probably forgotten more things than other vets had even learned. After thirty plus years with Uncle Pete, we were like family. Pete often told us we owned at least half of the clinic. When I look around Milliron I see Pete. There was the relaxed pastoral mood of the sheep in the meadows, the love of animals with cats, dogs, and horses everywhere. Going to Pete's was always an adventure and he didn't just care for our pets but he cared just as much about us. We could spend all day listening to Pete's tales about animals and people. So often when we had finished with an animal he would raise his hands and proclaim, "You are healed!" Now, Pete is healed in a different way and we miss him. Whenever we would lose a pet I would tell Pete, "The head may know and accept what is going on but the heart is slow to catch up." I feel the same way now.

Brandy
Raymond Abraham

Dr. Smith was my veterinarian for my dog Brandy. He was so conscientious with all our animals and gave such loving care. The entire Smith family remains my life-long friends. Jody, his wife, was very patient with me when I took Brandy to her obedience school. Jessica, his daughter, was a teachers-aide when I was teaching at Athens High School. Pat, his son, and his accounting firm were most helpful with the annual tax forms for my fraternity at Ohio University of which I have been alumni Advisor and House Director.

The first day I took Brandy to Dr. Smith, I was really impressed with his office and when I saw the large aquarium, I knew I would like him before I met him. The Smith family is an asset to our community.

Porky
Kylene Dunlap Brown

Pete was a traveling vet. He drove a Cadillac to do procedures that the vets here, in West Virginia, would rather not. He was real personable, he had a great sense of humor, and he liked to talk to people. He was my dad's vet, and that's why he was my vet.

Pete was always on the go. From Ohio to West Virginia, and everywhere in-between. I remember when Pete got a speeding ticket on Route 35. He wasn't happy about it, even though he was laughing when he told us he had gotten a ticket. I don't think it was his first.

My miniature pig "Porky" might have preferred a little more time before visits (Porky's trips to Milliron may have been considered stressful for Dr. Smith as well as patient) but somehow I don't think Pete minded.

Trucking a hundred miles one way to the clinic was never a chore. The clinic receptionist and vet techs would never tell Pete I was bringing the pig over because he never wanted to know that the pig was coming over. They used to say, "He heard the pig was coming over." Pete would grimace and say, "*Ooohhh.*" Then Pete remembered the food. I always brought food with me when I had an appointment. It seemed to help Pete's tolerance of my pig. I always brought two or three guys, one a rodeo clown, with me to help so Pete never had to do anything but what he had to do. Pete would always say, "How old is that pig?" I would say, "He's not old enough to die yet."

Being a part of Pete's Putnam County, West Virginia, delegation for some forty years, I'm selfish in thinking what I will do for a vet for my seventeen-year-old miniature pig that has only known Pete (and frankly wasn't that crazy about him). I'll never again hear him say to someone that their dog may be a rare breed called the "Catahoula Yard and Frog Dog."

Hocking College Intern
Katie Mace

I feel so blessed to have had Dr. Smith and everyone I worked with at Milliron in my life! It wasn't just work it was a family!

When I had to do my Hocking College internship, I decided I wanted to do it at Milliron Clinic with Dr. Smith and his staff. I had so much fun. I learned a lot from my time there. After my internship was through, I decided I wanted to volunteer and eventually Dr. Smith hired me.

I can still see Dr. Smith's smiling face and hear his contagious laugh. Just thinking of him makes me smile. I remember I was so afraid of not picking up on things quickly, or him not being very patient with me, but it was the complete opposite. He answered all of my questions and never hesitated to show me or anyone else how to do things.

Pete was a great teacher and a very influential person, not

only in Athens County, but other surrounding counties and states. He took such wonderful care of my horses! Lots of memories I wouldn't trade for anything!

Death of a Dog: for Sandy

Arvin Wells

We know that her death
    Was only a minute subtraction
    From the sum of things
We have almost everything left
    That counts in a human way ~
    Wife, husband, son and daughter
Soon we grow accustomed
    To her absence
    She will no longer haunt our halls
    With the click of her tags
She will take her allotted place
    In the larger perspective
    Of our lives ~ a happy memory
And so we can well afford the
    Little interval of grief we owe a creature
Who always did her best to respond
    To the mystery of our human needs
Who was tender and vulnerable and
    Idiotically in love with us all.

Cow Piles
David Sturbois

I called Pete for a farm call. My Hereford cattle needed inoculated. The cattle were all in my big box corral, crowded in there together, fidgety and being cows. Pete and I are in the corral, too, making our way through the herd. He's drawing out of the syringe and giving shots. I was marking the cattle as he inoculated them. Pete methodically approached each one and gave them a shot.

One of the cows made a sudden move and the syringe flew up in the air. It stuck in the ground, in a cow pile. Without hesitation, Pete bent over and pulled the syringe from the cow pile, wiped it off, and continued to use the syringe.

I said, "Are you going to sterilize that?"

Pete said, "Ordinarily I would, but that just happened to be a sterile turd."

Pete was practical about it. You can't change the needle every time you give a shot, especially under pressure.

Socks

Kathy Bowles

Dr. Smith's card acknowledging the death of Socks, my horse, meant much to me. I will never forget Socks. He was a good horse, a good citizen and gentlemen. I had high hopes that we would be able to enjoy his company for a couple more years, but this was not to be.

We realized that day, after Socks went down for the second time and stayed down, that we would have to let him go to better things. Socks did just that with the help of a compassionate vet. At times, I have wondered about compassion, and have come to understand that it is a constant flow that runs a little stronger when somebody needs to feel it in order to be able to go into the next day.

I learned yesterday from a friend that many horses are buried at Milliron Clinic, with room for more. The knowledge that so many gentle souls are laid to rest on Route 550 overwhelms me. I often question whether or not there is a Promised Land. I suppose I believe that it's everywhere – unnamed and unnoticed by many.

Some say the Promised Land is beyond a beautiful gate, with well-manicured lawns and streets paved with gold. As for me, I'll take the one with a little bit of broom sage, an old barn, and a gravel driveway going up the hill.

Vizsla
Lisa Toth Brosey

Pete has been our family's vet since 1975. Pete is number one in my book forever. You don't often find the compassion and dedication that ran through this man's soul. I am proud to have known him and have had him treat my animals. They broke the mold when they made Pete. He is greatly missed by human and animal alike.

In 2002, I came back to Athens from Upstate New York to visit my family at Easter. I brought my two Vizslas. One Vizsla had a surgical procedure done on her tail by my vet in Indiana. I had been struggling with the healing process. Finally, I decided to call Milliron Clinic to see if they would see her. When I went to the clinic, Pete and I began talking about the Vizsla breed and the problems with the breed, etc. I was telling Pete some of the stories from my Vizsla Club when he said, "Do you know why they have Vizsla Clubs?" I said, "No, why?" He wryly said, "It's a support group for other Vizsla owners." I laughed my butt off! By the end of the visit, we had the Vizsla in tip top shape and it wasn't anything a little silver nitrate did not take care of.

Another time I was living in Upstate New York and I could not find a vet to spay my Vizsla. She needed her teeth cleaned, too. The New York vet wanted to schedule two separate appointments for the two procedures, which was totally unnecessary. I just hated the *boutique* vet practices in our area. So, in the snow, I drove to Ohio, a nine-and-a-half-hour drive away. Pete's humor and smile were a warm welcome back to Milliron Clinic. Pete performed both surgeries with success. He charged me very little for the two surgeries, only $140.00! I almost hit the floor. My friends in New York thought I was crazy for taking my dog to Ohio for the procedures. If they could only witness how wonderful Pete was with both people and animals.

Muffet

Sunny Churchill

I always loved the mural at the clinic. In the spring of 2012, after Pete had passed, as I sat in the reception area, I glanced to the right. It seemed like Pete had walked through the gate in the mural and was standing between the horses by the tree. My eyes filled with tears, so, although the picture was a little blurred, I sensed that Pete had quite a welcoming committee when he passed on.

I had a similar experience at the Kentucky Horse Park. I was to meet Jody at the restaurant and we missed connections; one of us did not have our cell phone! I had never been to the Horse Park Museum and had no idea where the picture of Pete was displayed. Finally, I sat on a bench near an Arabian horse exhibit. As I looked ahead at a slide show, there was Pete smiling back at me! He was pictured sitting on a famous Arabian stallion. It was a beautiful day to be at the Horse Park, and although I did not meet up with Jody, I believe we each had an opportunity to sense Pete's presence.

On Thanksgiving Day 1991, Pete and his family offered to stop by our house in Bremen, Ohio, to euthanize our beloved sixteen-year-old dog, Muffet, on their way to Columbus. When it was time, Pete was most kind and compassionate. He had my daughter, Kerry, sit down and hold Muffet in her lap, so she would not be afraid. He explained that what he would give Muffet would ease her passing, and it did.

Afterwards, Pete, Jody, and Jessica hugged us and spoke words of comfort. When I got my purse, Pete refused payment and said, "It was my gift to help." The following week we received a sympathy note and a beautiful poem.

On a happier note, I always enjoyed opportunities to ride the trails on horseback with Pete. He was a special guide; considerate, observant, enthusiastic, full of fun. When we first stopped to visit, Jody asked if my daughter and I had time for a "short" ride before heading home to Bremen – this turned into a six-and-a-half-hour adventure! We ended up spending the night in our camper so we could ride in the morning with Pete.

Pete had a reverent way with animals; he loved and respected them. I had an opportunity to observe Pete doing surgery on my dog. He explained what he was doing, he blessed the animal and said a short prayer that it would run well. He also created a soothing environment and listened to classical music as he carefully worked.

He also told me about a horse he was going to put down. He explained it was a family pet whose injury could not be fixed. He gave me the opportunity to "talk" to the horse and explain that his family loved and appreciated him and that he would soon be out of pain. I gave the horse some grain to munch on while I groomed him. When it was time, I led him to a quiet secluded spot where Pete calmly gave him the injection. I felt humbled to realize how much Pete genuinely cared for the animals and the humans who loved them. I remember hearing him tell the family he was sorry the horse could not get better.

Baby Girl

Tina Dotson

On my calendar of events today it says *Call Dr. Pete to schedule yearly visit.* I gave up my vet where I live in Columbus, Ohio, when I decided to have Dr. Pete be my primary vet (something I will never regret). Now that Dr. Pete is gone, finding someone with his personality and knowledge is going to be a challenge.

I always put my full trust in Dr. Pete, never doubting him one bit. I always enjoyed the drive to and from Milliron Clinic and, of course, the visit with Dr. Pete and staff. I am sure a lot of people will wake up to a morning like this soon and wonder *What am I going to do?*

I was referred to Dr. Pete by Bud Strouss D.V.M. of New Albany, Ohio, and his companion Silvia, over four years ago. My toy fox terrier needed to have surgery on both legs. I drove the over an hour drive to Dr. Pete's and was very pleasantly surprised to meet such a wonderful person. His bedside manner and kindness stood out. He successfully did surgery on toy fox terrier, Baby Girl. I then decided to continue to see Dr. Pete for our primary vet. People often ask me why I would drive so far for vet care. I always responded with, "We love Dr. Pete; he is like part of our family."

On my last visit in November of 2009 to see him, he took the time to express sympathy to me for the passing of my mother. His gentle hug and kind words will never be forgotten. We feel privileged and honored to have had Dr. Pete take care of our beloved (toy fox terrier) Baby Girl.

King
Susann Williamson

There are so many stories of Pete's incredible wisdom and valor when it came to his large animal (horse) veterinary practice. From 1973, when he successfully repaired a spurting artery in my "King" granddaughter, three-year-old pleasure prospect's front foot to repairing a torn heel by casting it in 2009 on my current trail mare. The most amazing diagnosis was on my daughter's barrel horse, Tandy, who he actually diagnosed with ulcers just by simply watching him walk toward him across the parking lot from the trailer by the way he was chewing!!

I cannot say enough of Pete's willingness to serve us in time of need and often in great distress. We have been very fortunate to not need any emergency vet services over the past thirty-plus years of canine and equine ownership. But the last

131

couple of years have been the exception; the willingness and kindness of Pete's assistant, Ms. Rorick, to X-ray my dog, Zoey, while Pete was still in the hospital.

But, my favorite advice from Pete as to why we continue this "dirty habit" of horse ownership for now the third generation of girls is this: "Keeping a teenage girl on the back of a horse keeps her out from under a teenage boy." Well said, Pete, well said. As a born-again Christ follower and ardent prayer warrior, I believe my prayers were answered when I prayed for Pete's healing and my desire to see him again. Not in my selfish, physical way, but in the spiritual sense, knowing we'll spend eternity in Heaven retelling great horse stories!

Peacock and Laddy
Nancy Bonnette

Our son, Jamie, had a little dapple-grey Appaloosa pony named Peacock. One of our other horses kicked him and broke his leg. Pete said he couldn't do anything with him. He had tried to save the leg, but it was too mangled. The clinic and waiting room were full at the time. Jamie was sitting on the bench, the one along the inside wall. He was about four years old. We were all crying. Pete comes into the waiting room, kneels down and lifts Jamie onto his lap. With tears, Pete said, "I know you're just going to hate me. I can't save your pony." When we walked out, the entire clinic was crying. They didn't even know who Peacock was.

One Christmas Eve, when Jamie was about seven, we had a collie dog that needed surgery. The collie wasn't very well, he had it in the hips. Pete was steadying the collie's hindquarters while Jody was holding his head. The dog slipped on the table and bit through Jody's hand. It was a bad bite. The collie died. Jamie wanted to bring the dog home to bury. Pete had a casket built for the collie, placed the dog inside, and put a lock on it so Jamie couldn't open it. Pete said, "Jamie's going to hate me, but I haven't been able to save anything that he loves."

Pete used to say he had great intentions of being here early, and then he would always be late. "Well," Pete would say, "right down on US Route 35, I ran into a herd of pink elephants. You know you have to stop for them; you're not allowed to run them over." I always told him I didn't care what time he got here, I could get out of bed, and we have lights into the barn.

I went on farm calls with Pete when he was working in West Virginia. Jody would stay here and wash dishes and go to sleep. When we came back, Jody ended up driving back to the clinic because it would be like two or three in the morning and Pete would have to be at the office at nine. Pete taught me so much. He was our regular vet. The man was a genius, if the truth was known. He was like a brother to me. He and my husband, Jim, were good friends, too. He would pull in our driveway in his Cadillac. He had Ruffian, his dog, in the backseat. I called Ruffian the 'Roller Derby Queen' because she ran in circles in the backseat and tore it to shreds.

When Slim, an older gentleman who came to live with us, first met Pete, he asked Pete where he went to school. Pete said, "Colorado." Slim said, "By God that's why you're a damn good vet. You went out there to a school that knows what they're doing." Slim had an Australian shepherd that was ornery and didn't like Pete much. Pete wanted to have him castrated, but Slim just didn't believe in that. Slim said, "Nope, the Good Lord gave those to him, so he's got to keep 'em." There were times Pete would come in and said, "Hey, Slim! I won't charge you if you let me put that dog to sleep." Slim would smile and say, "You leave my Goddamn dog alone!"

My horse Laddy had been really abused. Everything bad that happened to him was because of men; he hated men. He would strike at them if he was out; try to get after them if they were near. I couldn't get a vet to work on him. I asked Pete to work on him once, and I told Pete that he hates men. Pete said, "Let's just go over to the barn and I'll turn and pat your arm, then you turn and talk to me, then talk to your horse, and we'll see what he does." I opened the stall door and Laddy didn't do a thing to Pete. He fell in love with Pete just that quick. Laddy trusted Pete. Pete used to go and bring an apple from the house. I always said, "You better take two apples." Pete said,

"That horse doesn't need an apple." Laddy would start looking in Pete's coveralls for the apple.

Pete was the first vet that told us that you could tranquilize a horse before you put them to sleep, and then they didn't know what was happening to them. The vets around here wouldn't do that. They just gave them a shot. One time one of the vets here tried to put down a horse with a shot, the horse just kept running around and around. Guess it must have lost its mind, or something. I think that it took the horse about 45 minutes to die. Pete said, "Well, yeah! You know you can give them a sedative, they don't know, they fall asleep, and then you just euthanize."

We had a red colt born that had the kinkiest, curliest hair, and he had a beard that was kinky, curly. He was a fine looking little fellow. I called Pete, just to be a smart aleck.

"Hey Pete! Guess what? I've got a baby!" I said.

"You do?" Pete laughed.

"Well, yes, it's my horse's baby, but it's mine!" I said.

"Oh my God, which mare had a baby?" Pete said.

"I think it belongs to you, it's got kinky, curly hair and a beard!" I laughed.

Pete couldn't stop laughing. He said, "Now don't tell Jody, we don't want this to get out."

Bitsy
Jared Butcher

Bitsy was a stray my wife and daughter brought home, she had been "sleeping" in the snow. I said, "Get that thing treated for every disease known to man."

Bitsy was brain damaged when they brought her home. She got progressively worse before pinworms were shown to be the problem. She would run in circles obsessively, and lick the air beside the bowl when you would try to feed her. Sometimes, she would run circles through the food dish, giving a combined effect the defines description.

On one particularly notable occasion, the family had gone to Parkersburg and left me at home. I was on the phone with my daughter's future mother-in-law when I noticed tracks in the fresh snow. Being certain that Bitsy was secure in her enclosure, I said something like, "Oh, look at the deer tracks."

That was stupid. Bitsy made those tracks by running in circles. My wife made my mistake clear to me when she got home, and the three of us commenced tracking the brain damaged dog. We picked out the freshest tracks and followed them. My wife followed the freshest racks around and around, but never caught sight of Bitsy – because Bitsy was following her.

Feeding Bitsy was not a treat. We would hold the bowl up and push her head down. On one particularly wintery day, Bitsy escaped her enclosure, and managed to make it out to US 50, where a kind soul stopped and took her to work with him. My older daughter was home from Ohio University just long enough to do a wash when she discovered Bitsy missing. Calling around, she found that a local business had the dog. When she arrived at the business, they spoke to her of dog abuse and threatened to call the authorities on account of the way she had been treating Bitsy. My daughter expected as much, and said, "At least let me feed her her breakfast." When they saw the extreme difficulty with which feeding was accomplished, they decided that it might just be the way things were, and they let my daughter bring Bitsy home and put her back in her pen.

We would need her actual records in order to list the maladies thrust on this brain-dead dog, but some involved medication, while others did not. I was the one who picked Bitsy up after surgery. Pete Smith came out to the waiting room to console me and explain about the surgery (I am the hardboiled one; his preparations were intended for my wife). He looked at me and said, "Well, I would say that this bodes well for you."

"Me?" I said.

"Yes, your wife won't be sending you to the County Home when the time comes," Pete said.

"What?" I asked quizzically.

"She doesn't have a *farmer's mentality*," replied Pete.

"What do you mean?" I asked.

"Look how she treats this dog. She's not going to abandon you because, well, look how she looks after this poor dog," Pete said, petting Bitsy's head.

"I see," I said.

"Now, a farmer will look at the field and say, *'Well, that ain't gonna produce'* and plow it under. Your wife won't do that to *you*," Pete continued.

At this point, we had spent a couple of thousand dollars on Bitsy, but it was worth it because, as I pointed out at the start, there were two patients. When Bitsy died, after eight years with us, Pete Smith let my wife cry on his shoulder. He understood that the important patient still lived.

Patty

Charlie Watson

I didn't know where the Milliron Clinic was or who Pete Smith was. Most veterinarians that you know are small animal vets.

It was 1984 and we were just getting into draft horses. When we found someone who knew about a big animal, we didn't even call anybody after that. We knew the difference between a good vet and a bad vet. Pete was a good vet.

I had big Belgian four-year-old mare, Patty, who had cut herself right below the knee, clear down to the hoof. She was a stunning mare, blonde with white mane, tail, and a stripe. I had no clue how Patty could have gotten hurt. I called Pete. "Is Pete around?" I asked. "No," said Karen, the receptionist. "He's in Colorado at a vet conference."

I had no other option but to call another vet. The other vet came on Monday and stitched Patty's leg and wrapped it, said to keep it dry, and to keep Patty in the barn. By Wednesday Patty's leg had swollen beyond the normal range. By then, Pete had returned from Colorado. I called Pete.

"I'll come up whenever I can get there," Pete said.

"Alright," I said, "but, I need you now."

Pete arrived at Charlie's in his big black Cadillac. The car was well-known throughout the region as Doris. Pete had a drugstore in the trunk. Pete walks to my barn and says, "Take that wrap off. Can she get up out of there?"

"I don't know," I said. Patty was in a stall that was on a lower level than the rest of the barn.

"Well, bring her up here to the other barn," Pete said.

By that time, my father-in-law, Herb, arrived and was helping to situate Patty so that Pete could work on her. Pete was busy preparing an IV. Pete told me to hold Patty and handed me the IV tube. He pulled out all the sutures from the first vet and re-sewed the artery and tendon sutures. While I'm holding the IV, Pete and Herb sit down on a nearby bench.

After a while, I said, "How long do I have to hold this Pete?"

"Until it's empty."

"Well, how long is that going to be?"

"About thirty minutes!"

"Thirty minutes!"

"Hold it a little higher, Charlie."

Patty's wound had become infected; that was why her leg was swollen, and you could tell she was in great pain. The IV now depleted, Pete got to work on the wound.

"Do you have anything that comes up above her knee that we could soak her leg in?" Pete asked me.

"Well, we got a plastic trashcan," Herb said.

"That'll be great. You got something you could put in there to stir the water?"

"A shopvac?" I asked.

"Yeah. That'll work. Put Tide detergent in the trashcan with some water. The wound has to be cleaned."

I filled the trashcan with a spray hose and brought Patty up to the trashcan, picked up Patty's foot. She didn't like it, deluging me with a trashcan full of water. Patty was a very, very large Belgian mare. She was gentle enough, but her size could intimidate the best horsemen. But she was used to me and trusted me, so I tried again. I sat the trashcan back up, picked Patty's foot up a second time and she put her entire leg down in the water. Pete told me to gently rub her leg.

"I want you to do it every day for three weeks."

"What?"

"Put her leg in there, and fill it up with water for thirty minutes, above the foot. Get your hand down in there and rub it; rub your hand up and down that wound."

Patty was doing very well, standing still in the trashcan of water and Tide. I told my father-in-law to go to the barn and bring back a scoop of feed. We dumped the scoop of feed in front of Patty, and then we hooked up the shopvac and inserted the hose into the trashcan, to create a whirlpool. Pete was sitting on the bench watching intently.

When we were getting ready to turn on the shopvac, Pete laughed and said, "Well, this will be the good part."

I stood beside Patty as the shopvac was turned on. Patty quizzically looks down at the water and jerks just a little bit. Herb and Pete continued a conversation while I was in an awkward position, arms in the trashcan, on my knees, rubbing Patty's leg for thirty minutes.

Days went by and Patty enjoyed the whirlpool; every other day for three weeks, then twice a week for an additional three weeks; nine weeks altogether. She liked it. She didn't want to get her leg out of the trashcan. Patty recovered completely and healed without a scar. It was one of the many innovative procedures that Pete developed during his lifetime: cost efficient, non-evasive, just plain commonsense.

We would call on our way down to the clinic and order a large pizza. We would order a vegetarian pizza for Karen, the receptionist at the front desk. We loaded up our horses, picked up the pizzas, and we would be the first at the clinic with our horses. We would all eat, especially Pete, and then he would work on the horses. Then, five other horse trailers would show up. We always tried to get there early so that we could be the first clients out, but Pete always saved my horses for last. "Oh, that's alright, they'll wait 'till last. They're family," Pete always said. I thought family meant that you could get in and get out.

On another occasion, I had a mare, Molly, who was pregnant and ready to foal. Every time I would take Molly to Pete for a checkup, the mare would have no milk. Pete told me not to worry about it. I was concerned, but Pete was emphatic. "Don't worry about it, Charlie. When the colt is born, the milk will come."

The colt was born; Molly had no milk. Friday afternoon, Pete and Jody, Pete's wife, made the farm call to my barn. Betty, my wife, had just come from the grocery store. Our farmhouse is on the side of the road, the barn is on the other side of the road. Jody and I walked over to the barn.

I looked around and said, "Where's Pete?"

Well, he had gone into the farmhouse. Betty just came in from Kroger's and had bought roasted chickens. He had eaten half a chicken before thanking Betty for the meal. Pete was carrying a box of oatmeal creams as he marched to the barn.

"Where have you been?" I asked him.

"I haven't eaten yet," Pete said.

Pete put his hand on the side of Molly and he looked her over and said, "You remember me telling you not to worry the milk would come when this foal came?"

I said, "Yeah."

"Now's the time to start worrying," Pete said.

Pete gave me the name of another veterinarian, Dr. Clyde Alloway. Dr. Alloway and Pete were friends and colleagues. With a regular dose of oxytocin, Molly's uterus contracted and within a week the colt was up and nursing.

After that Molly foaled two more colts. But on a March day, Molly was not doing well. She had foundered on new grass that spring. I told Pete that she was getting up like a cow and I had to give her a boost to stand. Pete said to bring her into the clinic.

Pete had always said that a horse could founder on air. I took Molly to the clinic, and Pete took a grinder and ground the horseshoe nails off, then pulled off her shoes.

Pete called and said, "Come and get her, I think she's fine."

Well, she kept going down and down. I had won the Ohio State Fair with Molly. I had many award-winning horses; county fairs and horse shows throughout Ohio and the surrounding states.

Pete was the one who told me about imprinting foals. I imprinted Rose, one of Kate's foals. Jody and Pete had read Dr. Robert M. Miller's book on imprinting. A graduate from Pete's alma mater, Colorado State University, Dr. Miller formalized the art of imprinting.

It was a rough birth—we had to pull Rose out of Kate. It was the same way that Secretariat was born. He got up real fast after he was born. Well, Rose was the same way. She was stuck in Kate. When we pulled Rose out, we busted her umbilical cord. We didn't stop until we hit the wall.

After Rose's traumatic birth, Pete immediately put her on the operating table. When it was all over and Rose was in recovery, I picked Rose's nose up and blew gently into it. After that, I would open the barn door and Rose would wait for me to blow in her nose before she would come into the barn.

Rose was fourteen years old when we lost her. She was out in the pasture. I sat beside her and she leaned forward and put her face on my chest. Her whole side was raw where she had been laying on that one side. She foundered just like her mother.

West Virginia Clover

Pam Rhule

I was so shy. Pete brought me out of it. He was so funny. He was dynamic. The first time I met Pete he came to tubeworm the horses, the old-fashioned way. He would come at one o'clock in the morning. I think he relished shocking new acquaintances. He inserted the tube down a mare's throat and said, "Yeah, she's full of worms." Well, I was amazed. He sedated the mare and told me there was a certain magic you had to use when you wake them up. He said words over them and *boing* they woke right up.

At one time, we had over forty horses. I was running a riding business. I had an agreement with my boarders that every horse that came into my stable had to have proof of shots and all the appropriate paperwork. Pete taught me to use my head and really think about things. I never minded Pete coming late at night because there was nobody at the barn at that time and we could get it done fast. He was there at ten o'clock at night one time to vaccinate horses. I still have the picture in my head—Pete coming to my barn in the middle of the night. He would drive up hill to my stables and into my horse arena. I always knew when Pete arrived. I would walk out to the arena and there would be a black faced dog peering out of Pete's car. It was the scariest thing in the middle of the night. It was a Stephen King sight. When we lived out on the dark road by the power plant, you could hear Pete coming before he ever got to the house because his shocks were hitting the ruts in the road. He didn't go slow. He went 60 mph on a road that had a 5 mph speed limit.

When we saw Pete coming up the hill, we would get our boots on and everything, and then Pete would pull in in that Cadillac. Every time I would say, "Pete, when are you going to get a new car?" Pete would say, "I don't know, when this one goes bad." He had the trunk tied with strings! He knocked the grill off of it one time when he came over. He tied it down with hay string. He probably lost it on our road! He said, "I got to get home, I got to get out of here." He was so tired. It was snowing. He runs out to his car, grabs the vaccinations, and has all the horses vaccinated in about thirty minutes.

Over the years I became accustomed to Pete's gestures

and characteristics. As soon as Pete came walking towards me grinning, I knew he was going to tell me a joke. I mean, you can't help but start smiling. I started laughing even before he told the joke.

Let me tell you this one story. This was just amazing. I had an old brood mare and she was not eating well. This is the first time I learned that a speculum meant everything when floating a horse's teeth. Pete said that every vet should use a speculum when floating a horse's teeth. Pete said to me often, "If you want your horse to live long, you'll have their teeth floated." The mouth speculum is a neat device. It has this leather strap and the metal goes into the horse's mouth so that the horse can't bite down. Pete said, "Stick your arm in there!" Well, my arm went clear to my elbow! Pete showed me that if you don't file a horse's teeth, they get these big old hooks. Pete said, "This mare has hooks. I'll try to get her here at your barn." Pete sedated the mare and used bolt-cutters to remove the hooks. He was having difficulty with one of the hooks and asked if I would hold the mare's head. Finally, he pulled the hook out. It was the size of my thumb! I was about seventeen at the time. I was amazed.

Pete would be in conversation, especially in the barn, working on horses. He was vaccinating my horses and I had one of my older students pull out the horses. It was like an assembly line. Pete would vaccinate one and then he would take the needle and throw it and it would stick in wood nearby. He always did that!"

One time Pete came down for my horses' spring shots. Jody was with him. My husband then would say, "Pete's wife is very quiet, isn't she?" I said, "She's the wing man! She has seen everything!"

Pete came to float one of my horse's teeth again, and Jack, my Corgi, got kicked by one of my horses. It knocked him out. Jack got up and he was slinging blood for a second. I asked Pete to look at him. Jack had a split tongue and a knocked-out tooth. Pete says, "Ah, he'll be ok." Anytime Pete said that, I knew it. I've never had him tell me that something would be ok and it wasn't. I knew that if he didn't tell me that it would be ok, then it was a problem. And Jack was ok.

Another time I had a mare, sold her, and traded her back as a yearling. Her legs were bow-leg when I got her back. Pete said the other owner had packed the protein to her and for some reason her cannon bone grew and the other side didn't. Pete put pins on the side that did grow, and then a cast. The mare was running in the pasture as a yearling with the brood mares with a cast on! She was fine! She finally passed for one of those long lines that I've kept forever. I've had many, many, many babies from her.

Pete could diagnose symptoms over the phone. The first time he diagnosed over the phone I remember it was raining. We had our horses in the lower barn. I was younger then. We had half doors where the horses could peep out their heads. You walk in the barn and there's six stalls—three on each side with their heads peeping out. When I walked in, the floor was soaked in front of all the stalls. I thought the water had leaked. It scared me to death. So, I looked around, went to get the grain to feed them and when they opened their mouth, water just dripped. I called Pete. "They've been eating clover," he said. "They will eat and then they will drink. Don't let them eat too much clover, or they will dehydrate." To this day, I know when my horses have been eating clover.

We had a mare that was having trouble. I got up one morning and her uterus had prolapsed. So, off to Pete we go. It was a bad time. My son sat with the mare in the trailer all the way to Pete's. He and she were the same age. They were raised together. We unloaded her at the clinic and Pete put her in the stall that had a lot of straw. We went back to see her and when we were leaving she nickered at us. I had her for twenty-four years. She died. It was so traumatic.

In later years Pete would look at me with his bifocals. His head bent and his bifocals sitting at the end of his nose and eyeing me over the top of his lenses. I'll never forget his face.

Bad for Business

David Sturbois

"Milliron Clinic, may I help you?" receptionist Karen chimed, answering the phone among barking, mewing, client interjections, the UPS man and mailman making deliveries, employees in and out, and the gurgle of the aquarium filter.

"I need to make an appointment for my dog. He needs his annual shots," local client David Sturbois said.

"Bring him in," Karen replied.

David eagerly entered the clinic, the dog was not so eager. It was a routine visit for yearly shots; parvo, tetanus, etc. The dog knew the smell and the aesthetics of Pete's office and was offended by the visit. No one knows for sure if the dog didn't like Pete, or if he just didn't like the clinic's cat, the one always on guard at the counter.

"Put him on the scale," directed Karen. "Sixty-five

pounds. You will be in Room 2."

Pete, in his signature light-green smock with the DVM Staff of Aesculapius on his left breast, met David in the examination room. They lifted the dog on the patient table.

"He might bite you, Pete," David said.

"Hold him still," Pete said confidentially, his mutton chops moving slightly.

The dog, struggling and wincing, found his head in David's lock hold while Pete administered the series of shots.

"Watch out!" David cried, as the dog drew a claw and slid it through David's left arm. Blood was running down David's arm as he gathered his dog and headed for the door.

"Try not to let anyone in the waiting room see you. It's bad for business," Pete demanded.

Living in the country in rural southeast Ohio is the perfect place to raise animals – and a family; knowing that Pete Smith was your vet made the venture more enduring. David decided to buy a cute little pony for his kids to ride. The pony was a little crazy and jumped through a fence, landing in some barbed wire, severing a major tendon in its hind leg. David had seen these kinds of injuries before and was doubtful the pony could be helped. Right away, David called Pete.

"Pete, I have this new pony..." David said.

"Bring her in," Pete said, sipping his daily dose of morning hot chocolate, "I can fix it."

Pete operated on the pony, using wires and screws to repair the leg. David took the pony home with a cast from hoof to hip. After several weeks, Pete told David to cut the cast off, knowing David had the wherewithal to perform the removal.

"How's the pony?" Pete inquired.

"You can't even tell that he had an injury; a magnificent surgical accomplishment. But the pony is just as stupid as ever," David replied. Pete completely understood.

Great Dane
Jerry Hartley

One complacent afternoon, a client brings a gorgeous Great Dane into Pete to be euthanized because it had bitten the son and wife. Previously another local vet had cropped the dog's ears, a normal request for the breed; however, the after-care of cropping a Great Dane's ears can be very painful for the dog if not handled properly. Pete was not a fan of the cosmetic operation. The owners had not followed the directions for caring for the dog's ears and they had used the wrong tape. The dog never forgot it; it was a terrible time for the dog. If the dog was asleep and your hand was near, the dog would remember the pain of the tape on his cropped ears and bite your hand.

"I have a friend who is wonderful with Great Danes," Pete said. "Would you like to see if he wants the dog?" The family agreed. The dog would have to stay in the clinic's kennels for a ten-day rabies observation while Pete contacted me.

I decided to take the Great Dane. We hit it off. We became well acquainted, I gave him a good life, if only for a short while. Four months later, I was lying on my couch watching football on TV. The dog was lying down on the floor in front of me. All of a sudden, the dog's teeth were in my face. Instinctively, I threw up my hands and the dog bit completely through my right hand.

I decided that the dog was too dangerous. I returned the dog to Pete to be euthanized. And so it goes in the animal realm. One must be cautious. Animal behavior is the direct result of human compassion and care; a mistreated animal can only hope to find solace in the hands of a caring veterinarian. Sometimes physiological damage cannot be reversed. Pete was known for placing the right pet with the right owner. He always avoided euthanizing, if possible.

Pete had this dartboard mounted on the wall in the large prep room. Every time he would go out there, he would have a syringe in his mouth and he would do whatever and then he would flip it. Every time it hit the dartboard. He could throw it clear across that room, 30 feet. *Fling. Boing.* Right in there. The dart always hit the mark every time. They always landed backwards every time I tried it. I don't know how he did it. He could throw in any gauge; big needle, little needles; big syringes, little syringes. It always stuck.

Hank

Randy and Becky Pierce

We became acquainted with Pete in the early 70's when we got our first horse. I can still see him backing his Cadillac in the drive and seeing his dog sitting in the backseat. No matter how big or small the problem was, he always took it seriously. He had such a passion for animals that it was like an aura around him.

When we bought our Quarter Horse stallion from Iowa, he caught pneumonia. Pete came out, mixed some medications in saline solutions, threw the rope over the rafter and gave it to the horse by IV. Sure did the job! Hank lived to be seventeen n years old.

He saved more than one animal for us over the years. There were many times I had to call him after hours, but he never complained. He was a vet who didn't make you feel like he was in a rush to get you out of the office and explained things in terms you could understand. When we received word of his passing, we felt we had lost not only a vet, but a good friend, too. God apparently needed a 'special vet' for all the loved pets that are in heaven! No one can replace Pete! Gone but never forgotten.

Harley

Robin Neville Rogers

The very first time Pete came over to our farm, Harley associated Pete with that first visit and Harley waited for Pete at the gate every time. Every time Pete came, we would have to muzzle Harley. He was the gentlest dog in the whole world, but he was afraid of Pete. But Pete would come driving up in his Cadillac. There's this song, I don't know if you've heard it, Chris LeDoux sang it, it's called *Cadillac*. We always think of Pete when we hear that song - *10-4 good buddy, come on back, horse trailer on a Cadillac.*

Pete was honest. You knew where you stood with Pete. He always told us that we put the fun in dysfunction. When we would go to the clinic, the vet tech would say, "Oh, there's Harley again." You know when you go in the door, the little exam room on the very end, to the left, straight back. One weekend we took Harley to the clinic. We set him up on the examination table and waited for Pete. Pete walks in, Harley jumps off the table, takes off, gets under the refrigerator, turns the refrigerator over to try to get away from Pete.

Eyeing the upended refrigerator on the tile floor, Pete quickly tranquilized Harley, "I'll be back in a minute after the tranquilizer works on him."

After the appropriate time, Pete came back into Harley's examining room and Harley's still not under. Pete leaves and returns fifteen minutes later. Harley's flipping his tongue out and going berserk. "Ok, someone get a muzzle on him, we got to get him clipped," Pete sighs.

All we were doing was clipping his toenails! I had my cat, two dogs, and my two horses there that day. But Pete just took it in stride. All available hands held onto Harley; Pete clipped his toenails, put him in a cage, and then he went on to do all my other animals. We load up our two horses in the horse trailer, the cat and dog, pays the bill and starts to leave when one of the vet techs said, "Hey, you left your dog."

"What dog?" I asked.

"Your shepherd!"

"I don't have a shepherd!"

Pete came out in his doctor's coat and said, "Look, I am not keeping this dog. You have to take the dog with you!" Laughing at Pete, I get Harley and put him in the car. Since

Harley could be a handful, Pete prescribed St. John's Wort. Pete said it was like Prozac to a dog. It worked. Harley slept the entire trip home to West Virginia, and then some. It was hours before the tranquilizer wore off and Harley was free to dream of visiting Milliron Clinic once again.

Once, my dog needed surgery. A local veterinarian estimated the surgery would cost $2,699. I called Pete, who said the surgery would be about $500.

Other vets didn't do the surgeries that Pete did, nor did they have the facilities. We traveled a long way to Milliron Clinic for expert vet care. Even if Pete was busy, the girls would go back and get him. We liked Pete's whole staff. We took one of our dogs to Pete and left him there for diagnosis. Pete called me and said, "You need to come over here. Your dog has leukemia." I drove to the clinic, called off work, and sat there from six in the morning until seven that night. I sat there and held my dog in his cage all day. The vet techs and clinic workers worked around me. I am sitting there holding my dog when Pete said, "You are the most selfish person I know. He's suffering and you want to sit and hold him. You just go right ahead and hold him, and when you think he's suffered enough, you let me know and I'll come back. I'm going to go home and have some dinner, then I'll be back to lock up." That evening, when Pete returned, I let my dog go.

Whistler
Mimi Hart

The amount of time I spent sobbing in Pete Smith's arms is a lot. But I also spent time sobbing in his staff's arms - Karen's arms, Jan's arms, and Jody's arms. Pete was just starting out and establishing a place when I met him. Pete was bigger than life. He was a big charismatic guy.

The first thing I have in capital letters is 'staff.' Pete and his partners; Pete hired some of the best people around. The staff was remarkable, the continuity was great; the fidelity, the love, the warmth. I always admire people who hire the right people. Even on a joyful day we hoped things would be all right; to feel the support of that environment. To drive over that bridge and to hear that cattleguard.

Even on the most optimistic day; a long life is ahead of you with any pet. To have that kind of "take in a stray attitude." To all of us who went to Milliron Clinic, it was like problem solving. Sometimes the problem was that you had to have an animal put down, but you knew you were welcome. Pete cared that your animal was going to be treated well. Sometimes it was going into something familiar. The sound of the cattleguard has registered grief to me many times.

I've been here as long as Pete has. I was among Pete's first clients. I was young, stupid, as were my friends. We were so naïve. He was just starting out and establishing a place. We found him, a group of my friends and I. We were just poor, struggling young people, trying to make our way. A bunch of us lived together. There was another vet in town that we had been to with my cat, who I didn't like. Then I heard about this new guy in town, out in the country.

We had a lot of animals. I had a pet goat, a couple of goats actually. They were goats that someone was going to butcher, and we said we would just take them. My first goat's name was Horton. He was like a pet dog. He went for walks in the woods; just like asking my dog. He was a Nubian goat with a broken horn, and we had him fixed. We went on and had a couple more goats, but like I said Horton was our first goat. He was like a pup. He would break into our house, rip out the screen, and eat the mail. He loved to eat sweat. If you were sitting on the lawn on a hot day, he would come up and lick you up like a salt lick. Horton would try to climb my apple tree to eat my apples. We had him for years. Horton got old and faded away. When Horton died, Pete cremated him for us. It was a horrible thing. Pete was so patient. We took Horton's ashes home.

None of has had grown up with farmyard animals, here we were living on a farm, five of us living together, $17 a month; we could barely afford the animals. That was another thing, Pete would always accommodate us and charge us $10, or so.

One of my girlfriends bartered for vet services. She had a dog named Booger. Booger was a long-hair, white-mix of who-knows-what, a big dog. Pete called dogs like Booger *Appalachian Porch Hounds*. Booger loved groundhogs. He had been hit by a car two days earlier. My girlfriend made Pete a cowboy shirt with piping in exchange for vet services. It was a brown and white print with a western theme, for a horse riding dude. That's the thing about Pete, he was willing to barter.

One time I was out to the clinic. I had been going to grad school and I was living alone at the farm. Pete said, "You need a dog. I think you need a dog and I have a dog here that someone dropped off. It's a little circus dog and you need to take him home." So, he gave me a dog. I told Pete that I had never had a dog. I was so paranoid about the dog. I was gone so much, but of course my neighbor fed the cats for me. I had dogs, but they weren't my responsibility, coming home from this life after being on the road for twenty some years, going to graduate school, writing papers and I didn't even know how to type. So, my whole world was new. Exciting, but new. But Pete said I need to take home this dog today. I did. The dog was amazing. His name was Whistler, he was my first dog. It was a *wonderful* decision. He was a little black terrier mix and I took him sight unseen. Whistler would keep raccoons out of the pet door, and all of the things we needed a dog to do.

Eight years later, I had friends in from out of town. I was caring for their dog. They were turning into the farm and unloading their luggage. The car was my husband's car, he had given it to me, it had electric windows; I never had electric windows in a car before. I had just come from the airport, and I had all this luggage; a girlfriend who is really high maintenance and all that. I said, "Where is Whistler?" Whistler had jumped in the backseat of the car, which he always did. The car windows were up and Whistler wasn't breathing. I got in the car and drove Whistler to Pete. It takes forty minutes to drive to the clinic, and that's on dirt roads. I sobbed in Pete's arms and said, "What can I do. Reanimate him." Pete said, "I can do a lot for you, but I can't reanimate him." He was dead.

I sobbed in Pete's arms. He had given me the dog. Whistler was my absolute friend. He was joyful and friends loved him. I have a great portrait of him in front of my neighbor's house. He would go down there to make sure that wild animals hadn't taken over this old house. Since, my neighbor's house has fallen into disrepair and my darling dog is gone.

My stories of Pete are very personal, like the story of my dog. I had a wonderful relationship with Pete. We loved each other. I told him I loved him. Part of his beauty was that he made individuals feel special. We all loved him, except for those of us who didn't love him. Some people were turned off by that big personality.

I can tell you Pete was not always sentimental. Those of us who love animals are victimized by those who abuse them. There were a number of cats dumped on our farm. One stray cat I named Jed. I brought Jed to Pete and he said, "Just put it down, it's a stray." Pete wasn't sentimental about how many feral cats there are. Karen, the receptionist at the clinic said, "You can save this cat, Pete. You can do it, nobody else can do it." Then the next day when I went to the clinic, Pat, Pete's son, happened to walk in. He said, "Is that your cat? That's the ugliest cat I've ever seen." I said, "Don't say that. You've been here all your life and you've seen ugly cats." Pat said, "Yup, but that's the ugliest."

Zoo-Zoo
Jared Butcher

Zoo-zoo was a lovely cat and passed many uneventful years until, close to the end of his life, he got urinary tract infections that are characteristic of neutered males. On one particularly memorable visit, Pete Smith spoke, more like shouted, to me that I must immediately stop serving him the brand of cat food I was using, it had too much ash, etc. The cat food was not the only problem, and the infections recurred again and again. It was awful. Eventually Pete Smith was at his wits end and he told me, man-to-man, "The only thing left is to amputate his penis—he won't be needing it anyway."

I cringed, but, solemnly, agreed. It was a tough sell, but eventually everybody in the family agreed. Zoo-Zoo was not consulted, he wasn't a voting member, but he had an opinion. The surgery was beautifully executed, and all went well. A catheter ensured that there was no damage to the remaining parts during the healing phase, etc. The time came to remove the catheter before the troubles started. The catheter would not release; or, Zoo-Zoo would not let go and release the catheter; the catheter had to come out, you understand. The way I remember it: They, meaning Pete Smith and an assistant, had Zoo-Zoo in a bag like a mail pouch because there are certain stressful situations in which a fellow is forced to defend what little bit of himself remains. Anyway, Pete Smith and Zoo-Zoo needed a moment alone with the assistant, so the three of them disappeared into a backroom. There was very little for my daughter and me to do, so, we listened. Echoing from the back came the most awesome scream a cat can produce. Moments later, Pete Smith came back.

"Did you get it?" I asked.

"Did I get it?" Pete Smith asked.

In my memory, Pete Smith is walking toward me wearing an apron and carrying the bag that contained the cat. His apron is adorned with a splash of yellow shaped like "Spin Art" gone wrong. Pete Smith is saying, "Did I get it? Did I get it?" I kept saying, "I got it." It might be my imagination, but, I remember a satisfied look in the cat's eye. Removing the penis had the desired effect, but the urinary tract infection was only the start of a downhill spiral in Zoo-Zoo's health. He had bouts in which he lost control over his bowels, and, offended by the smell, he would run to get away again, and again. This resulted in the uninhabitable room and an excrement covered cat. My wife would clean up the room and wash the cat, as needed, for about a year.

On one particularly noteworthy occasion, she called to me, "Jed, I need you to hold the cat." Zoo-Zoo was in the bathtub in an aggressive state of mind. He lashed out, and, sank his claws in my arm such that they penetrated my flesh on the way in and on the way back out. I said, "He's got me. He's really got me." But he didn't want me. "What do you want me to do?" my wife asked. I didn't know. She didn't know. Zoo-Zoo didn't know. All he knew was that I had him by the scruff, and he had me by the arm. My wife pressed on his paw and slipped the claws back out the way they had come. I washed, lanced, bleached, and washed—it never got infected. Zoo-Zoo eventually died from cancer, but the tenderness with which Pete Smith handled the grief expressed by my wife and daughter is without equal. He knew he had three patients, and he loved them all. He was a gruff old bird, but he loved all of us, and we loved him.

That's No Bone

Larry Hines

The first time Pete was to our farm, we had some calves that had pinkeye. Pete went out in the pasture with a rope and dropped the calves, rolled their eyelid back, put some dexamethasone in their eye, and gave them shots in all their eyes. That was the first time I met Pete. The next time he was to our farm, we had a cow that had cancer – that's what Pete said when he first saw the cow. He was exactly right. We had her in the barn and my dad was going to kill her. Pete said, "Oh, no, don't let that happen. Just let her die on her own."

We had calves we were feeding in the barn for the Athens County Fair. Pete pulled a quart of blood out of each calf and gave it to the cow with cancer. He would mark each calf so that he didn't draw twice from the same calf. When the cow did pass away, we kept Pete down that night, it was about midnight, and posted her (necropsy). He showed us what cancer looked like. He was interested in cattle and worked a lot on our cattle when he first came to Athens.

I took horses over to him, too, to Milliron. He bred horses for me using AI (artificial insemination). He would check a stud horse's semen for me to use for AI. Pete done it all. He cut a lot of horses for me, too. He did a whole bunch of stuff. I was over to Milliron Clinic a lot. We spent a lot of time together. I helped him and he helped me. There was none around like him, I'll tell you that. And there never will be really. I could go over with my draft horses and Standardbreds anytime.

I had a bull one time. I was at the stock sale and my son called me and said that the bull was limping really bad. I told him to put him in the chutes, pull his foot up and take a look. He said it looked like the bone was coming out of the bull's foot. When I got back, I took the bull to Pete. Pete grinned, "No, that's no bone, let's just pull that out of there." He pulled it out. It was a tooth of a two-year mare.

The Wolf Fighter - The Vole Slayer
Victoria Goss

Pete was always a favorite dinner guest at my house. He and Jody were regulars whenever we felt like really "Putting on the Ritz"! There would be good food, wine and laughter, and then, of course, *stories. Do Tell!!* The story of this particular dinner became a legendary tale... actually two!

On the menu that night was Tornados Roccini, a French dish *involvoign demi-glace* (a rich reduction sauce that could bring the dead back to life, make a simpleton comprehend, and the unfortunate in appearance fortunate indeed), filet mignon and a bunch of other European fancy stuff. I put on my finest table with all the little niceties that make it perfect: starched linens, fine china, crystal stemware, real silver, etc., all the wonderful things that I acquired the knowledge of in my New England upbringing and, of course, in finishing school.

When people meet me and see where I live, they can't believe that somewhere in the bowels of my moldy cabin lie such treasurers as these in repose, or that somewhere under the crusty exterior that is me there might dwell the dignity and class of an old style New England blue blood. I guess we all make choices. There is something whole, something religious, something Zen about preparing a beautiful table to compliment the beautiful food that complements our beautiful friends, creating for them an experience, not just a meal. So, yeah, every once in a while I like to "French it up"!

There we were enjoying a lovely repast and having a belly full of laughter – about eight of us in all. At this point, I feel that I have to break into the story and go back a couple of steps to introduce you to a missing member of the party, an uninvited guest: The Wolf.

Yes, he was a real flesh and blood wolf. Not some namby-pamby hybrid (I had those, too), he was the real deal. Man, oh man, I could tell you some stories about him, but that's another book. Well, he was a rescue, he had been taken out of the wild in Canada, illegally as a puppy, and some guy was raising him in a cage, in the back of a van, in Florida. This nut job was feeding him a strictly vegetarian diet in the hopes of creating "a kinder, gentler wolf." Long story short—he was losing control of the animal and couldn't deal with him any longer. They were going to put him down... or... yeah, yeah, yeah.

He was not unlike having a special needs child. There was the matter of constant supervision, learning wolf and creating a pack. We were very successful with him... but not without a great deal of effort. He was and would always be a wolf—the Wolf, until, at age 15 and a half, after a series of debilitating strokes, Dr. Smith set him free from the constraints of his earthly form.

At the time of this dinner, however, there was nothing debilitated about The Wolf. Everyone who knew us knew their way around him, respectfully so. Jody didn't cotton to the wolf - not one teeny, tiny little bit. Every time she saw him or me, she felt compelled to fill me in on the danger he presented to everyone around him. Jody would really get intense about it... what was I to do? He was kind of thrust upon me and I accepted the responsibility and made a commitment to him. I guess we all make choices.

So we have The Wolf tip-toeing around the house (they are quiet, shy creatures), more than a couple of "leery" dinner guests keeping one eye on the move for The Wolf and The Dinner Party.

When Pete Smith finds a food that he likes he will eat it— he will eat it until he no longer can. This delicacy will either be gone or Pete will no longer be able to swallow another bite— this was the case with Tornados Roccini. This was his second time enjoying this particular dish at my house. Upon arrival, he announced that he was prepared to not only unbutton his jeans, but his shirt as well, if necessary! As it turns out, filet mignon with a sauce that is the reduction of two cows and four sheep, served on thin slices of toasted sourdough bread and topped with a thin layer of fois gras was also found to be beyond the range of resistibility to The Wolf. He was lingering close to the party, bathing in the aroma, nearly floating on the hypnotic vapors.

Right around this time Pete, as promised, unbuttoned his pants and reached for another serving of Tornados Roccini. As the old saying goes… "there's many a slip twixt the lip and the cup"… and somehow Pete's tenderloin landed on the rug. As he headed for it with his fork, so did The Wolf, packing his own sharp, pointy objects. They both froze, staring at each other for a moment, at an equal distance from the meat. The Wolf silently raised his lips, revealing his sharp, pointy objects, just in case this human had momentarily lost its mind and needed a wake-up call. Right then Pete made a *raaahh* sound and faster than a slide show magician had the meat resting on his plate. The Wolf turned and slid back into the shadows.

It really wasn't a huge confrontation - my Grandma could have made that domestic wolf back off in her sleep! Still, given the circumstances, many a candy-pants customer would have let The Wolf have it. The circumstances being this: the meat fell on the *rug*, not just any rug; *my* rug. I wouldn't even sit on the rug fully dressed! I have raised puppies and kittens on that rug. I have been a willing participant in the non-stop abuse of that rug by manure-covered boots... for years. The cats and dogs have used that rug for their post-mortem theater for time infinitum!! Do you think it's ever been cleaned? NO! Pete knows these things. I broke the silence of these last few intense moments...

"You're not going to eat that after where it was?"

"I fought for it, I'm going to eat it," Pete said. "To the victor go the spoils!"

And the laughter once again breaks across the table like a tsunami; another story of Dr. Smith's ferocity in battle for the books. But wait... oh, you betcha there's more. About an hour later I spot a mouse on one of the logs that make the wall of the cabin in which we are dining, by candlelight. It's a smallish *juvenile* mouse. In anger (I hate mice), being an opportunist (it's on the wall) and I guess because my lack of decorum won't let known vermin slide, not on my watch, I react. "Look at that little mouse," I say, and I struggle to my feet, take one of my crutches (did I mention my broken leg?), and I was going to smash that little mouse with the bottom of my crutch. Pete gently grabs my arm to lower the crutch. "Don't do that," he said. At this point I was so embarrassed by the fact that I could not control my blood lust, even in the face of a formal dinner! I sat back down with some "I'm sorrys," "yer rights," and probably some very quiet "what was I thinking" only to see Pete pick up his butter knife, look over his bifocals and with a quick flick of the wrist, send that mouse to his destiny. He never moved from his chair or even took aim. By the time the butter knife catapulted towards our little mouse, he was on (in) a sculpture that I had made involving bones and twisting branches, not even remotely representing an easy target—but I'll be damned. The butter knife found its mark! The mouse and knife fell to earth—never having touched the sculpture. The entire room was going crazy—you couldn't have slipped a cannon blast in and heard it! What a shot! Unbelievable!

So casual and unassuming was this debonair marksman's demeanor. In nearly no light, from a distance of nearly ten feet, sideways to the target, and through a maze of twisting sticks and bones, with a butter knife, and virtually no aiming. I'm telling you, this was a million-to-one shot! Peter pulled it off. There was quiet talk around the table of The Mighty Vole Slayer. It was the most amazing thing anyone had ever seen.

Really, it was. Even Pete was amazed.

I took the mouse to a taxidermist and had it set standing on its hind legs with over-sized claws and teeth. Mounted under it - the very butter knife, etched with one notch, and a plaque "Pete the Vole Slayer" - it wasn't just a *mouse*! That trophy spent the rest of its days on the wall of Pete's equine exam room. He would greet customers at the door, with a proud display of mighty claws and saber-like teeth (just in a particularly diminutive state).

I could probably write at least a couple of volumes of stories that Pete told me about himself and perhaps another on our exploits. I was honored to be called friend.

Shaking Lambs

Pat Smith

I had this friend who I introduced to this really good-looking friend of my wife, Karen. Cheryl and Karen were best friends in elementary, middle and high school. Cheryl was a teacher in Tampa, Florida, at that time. She was back home to visit and we are all out for dinner. Cheryl said, "I would like to meet a guy, thirty-years-old, never been married, no kids."

This guy who works for Ohio University walks in. He worked for the athletic department, he's thirty-one-years-old, never been married, no kids. Cheryl is just drop-dead gorgeous, and Vinnie is very Italian, really good-looking. I walk over and I said, "Vin, would you like to meet someone?"

He said, "Who...?" I introduced them, they hit it off from the beginning. I had to leave because my boys were at a hockey game, so I left Karen and Cheryl with Vinnie. He took them home that night. Cheryl was staying at our house.

Later, Vinnie and Cheryl were married and now they have two little kids. They were back visiting Milliron Farm one day and it was lambing season. They wanted to see the little lambs. We took them up on top of the hill by the farmhouse, and I said, "This is a great time because we've got a ewe trying to have lambs right now. My dad is on his way now to pull the lambs."

Cheryl and Vinnie look on as my dad, Dr. Smith, reaches inside a ewe, pulls out a lamb, and puts it right into Vinnie's arms. Dad said to Vinnie, "Take it, take it!"

Vinnie's eyes got big. Dad said, "*No! Shake it*! Shake it between your legs!"

Vinnie is freaking out, he has blood and mucus all over him. Vinnie shakes the lamb. Dad grabs it away from him, shakes the shit out of it, and hands it back to him. Dad said, "Keep shaking it!" Then he reaches down and grabs another one and hands it to Vinnie, too. Vinnie's like '*UUhhh...*' Dad takes the one that Vinnie had and it was dead, then he tosses it over his shoulder and said, "Here! Shake this one!" Then Dad goes in and grabs the third one. He's shaking it and Vinnie's shaking the other one and this little lamb gasps for air and lived. Vinnie starts crying. He said, "I birthed a lamb!"

I've seen him about ten times since then, and every time I see him he tells me that story.

Smoothie

Jerry Sullivan

Smoothie was a sorrel five-year-old Quarter Horse with a broken back femur. She was a prize mare of a client from West Virginia or Kentucky. They used her for barrel racing or some kind of cowboy stuff. I worked for Pete when they brought her in with a completely convoluted femur; I mean it was an open fracture. She had stepped into a groundhog hole.

We prepped Smoothie for surgery and put her on the large hydraulic table. Her surgery was complicated and took a very long time. Pete pinned, plated, and screwed her leg back together.

Smoothie wasn't able to put weight on her leg after the surgery. Pete had a special belly-band made for her and hung her in a stall. We hung her so that she could touch the ground occasionally, on a pulley. She was in the third stall on the left.

Her owners kept in touch with her. They realized it was a

high-risk surgery and the odds weren't in Smoothies favor.

Smoothie was a wonderful horse. We spent a lot of time adjusting the weight of the apparatus and changing the center balance so she would be comfortable.

After about six weeks, she wasn't getting any better. The bones were not grafting together as Pete anticipated. When I let her down very gently, her leg just popped and came apart.

Not only was I working at the clinic then, but I was living there, too, in the apartment Pete had above the clinic stables. I was always available if Pete needed anything. One morning, Pete called me at 1 a.m. and said, "How's Smoothie?" I said, "Oh, she's here." Pete said, "Let's let her down." And I said, "You sure?" And Pete said, "Yeah."

I was heartbroken. I had spent hours with Smoothie; grooming her and giving her medication. I had an emotional connection with her. I spent a lot of time like that after Vietnam; screwed together and hung up in a bed due to a war injury. Fortunately, mine grew back together, but Smoothie's never did.

Deworming the Sheep
Leslie Savage

One of my favorite stories about Pete is deworming the sheep. We were on a long Ohio Horse Council horseback ride around the Milliron Farm culminating at Windy Hills, right across the road. Pete told a story on himself that day about deworming the sheep. He said one day when they were working on the sheep, he had wiped the sweat away from his forehead with the sleeve of his shirt. Later, he experienced excruciating pain in his eye. The eye doctor at the local hospital in Athens examined his eye and reported to Pete that a worm had latched into his eye, hooked in! It was from when he was de-worming the sheep! There was nothing they could do about it. I don't know whether Pete mulled it over or decided then, or on the way home, but when he got home, he wormed himself with a dose of ivermectin, and it killed the worm. His eye pain went away.

The reason this is one of my favorite stories about Pete is

because it shows a lot of important elements that made Pete who he was; matter of fact, straight forward, clear as a bell, not giving up, finding a way, technically, physically, mentally, and spiritually proficient as a person, using everything, thinking of things the doctors didn't think of, having the confidence to try ivermectin, and I bet he planned for contingencies he didn't have to use in case the ivermectin didn't work. But, we don't know his contingency plan because of his being matter of fact which cut down on unnecessary talk.

Don't Bring That Mule Back
Ernie Antle

I liked to work with Pete. We got a group together to clean horseback riding trails out to Stroud's Run State Park. There are trails there named after Pete. Of course, Pete knew that I always carried four or five sandwiches. There was about four of us cutting the trails. We ate real good that day. Pete always ate someone else's lunch if he didn't have any food.

Pete was my sister Sherry's vet. We had an Irish Setter. We're dog and horse people. Pete would always call and say, "You got to have something to eat." He would stop at my sister's place because she is one fantastic cook. She always fed him when he came through, so he always knew he was going to get something to eat.

We were getting ready to go to Tennessee and we needed vet papers. We brought our mules to Milliron Clinic. Pete has a metal stanchion in the prep room. Jim, another buddy of ours, has this little mule. Pete brought the needle out and the war was on. That little mule got underneath one of those bars and froze right up and hit that bar. Pete more or less said when Jim left, "Don't bring that mule back."

One thing you could say about Pete, he liked to horseback ride hard. If it was a Pete Smith trail, he took it. Pete said there was a guy who worked for him who would talk about American Saddlebred horses as fancy-peacock horses - that they weren't worth anything. Pete said, "You don't know these horses. John Wayne rode an American Saddlebred." Of course, John Wayne rode Saddlebreds without their tail broken or anything.

When we would go over to the clinic, Pete told me that he went over to Brazil. I said, "Boy, Brazil must have some fancy horses." He said, "Believe it or not, I think the Standardbred is as much athletic, smarter, and easier to train than other breeds."

Cryptorchids

Tracey Thiele

The very, very first time I met Pete, I had a Paso Fino stud colt that I bought. I hired Dr. Strouss to come down and geld him. I made one mistake when I bought him, I kind of glanced down there, but I forgot to count...one, two... The worst thing was the guy I bought him off of, well, we spent at least an hour talking about cryptorchid horses. He never once mentioned to me that this stud colt only had one testicle that descended. He lied to me.

Dr. Strouss came down to geld him. Before he came I looked under there and I said, "Uh, oh, we have a problem." There was one testicle, not two. Dr. Strouss set up an appointment for me to take him down to Pete's clinic. I had never been there before, and I had never met Pete. We drove down with my horse and I told Pete my story. He said, "No problem." He had to go clear up into the horse's flank. The testicle was really buried. Pete had to do table surgery on him. He just couldn't get it to come down, it was buried in there.

Pete loved to talk. He told me how he came to Ohio because of the beautiful scenery in the Ohio Valley and the local university. He told me that over 50% of his business was doing cryptorchid horses. That people sent them in to Milliron Clinic from everywhere to have their cryptorchid horses vetted. I took a horse to the clinic for my girlfriend; I took another one of mine, then another friend took two of horses to Pete. We seemed to get a lot of cryptorchids.

I had a mare named Lahoya, she was foundering. I took her down to Milliron Clinic. When we got there, Pete was looking at her, and she was in the very beginning stages. He said that he had tried this before and he thought it would work. He was going to give her an IV and he told me it was his own special concoction, that it was garlic oil, and whatever else. I believed him. He gave her an IV and she just stunk like you wouldn't believe. I went home and I am telling everybody that Pete has this wonderful concoction, because my mare was doing really well. I am sure it was Sylvia Snabl who informed me Pete was pulling my leg. It was just plain DMSO that he put in her IV. She smelled for a long time.

Blackberry Cobbler

Kay Williams

It was never a dull moment with Pete. Pete was really good. I've known Pete since I was sixteen. I was going to go to school to be a veterinarian. Pete said, "You know if you go to school to be vet, maybe you can work with me."

We have all kinds of Pete stories. I would call up and say, "Pete, I need some advice." And then I would tell him to send me a bill for all the advice. He said, "Just make me a blackberry cobbler." He liked to eat.

He always had a joke for you and he never got in any hurry. I've been in horses for about fifty-three years, there wasn't anyone more knowledgeable than Pete. It didn't make any difference, what state or where you were, you just mention the name Pete Smith. People either knew him or knew who he was. We were always calling Pete for information. We kind of had this thing between us.

It seemed that people would bring horses to Pete as a last resort. If a client could stand the sight of blood, they could watch surgery from the clinic hallway window. It was policy, at least at other vet clinics, that no one, no owner, no trainer, not anyone, even the referring vet, watch surgery. I always thought that was a little weird.

Pete always worked us in. Pete always suggested charcoal and yogurt. We had a newborn baby a week early. She was just gorgeous. The mare that night was up and down and up and down. Finally, we gave her an injection. The baby was fine. We went down to our stables one night and the mare's bowels wouldn't move. We gave her an enema. It really didn't work. She would get up and fall down. I thought we were going to lose her. She was really worth a lot of money, so, we gave her another enema. We stayed up with her until 11:30 that night. We got up the next morning; she had straw all over that stall, bouncing off the walls, kicking and everything. We gave her some yogurt and she was fine. Pete helped us a lot. Pete would give the horses DMSO. I'm not kidding you; don't go down to the barn for three days because it's like, *hold your nose*!

Pete used to work on our cattle. Before he quit that, I took a bunch of calves up there to have them castrated. I said, "How come it's only $5 a piece to castrate those calves, and dogs and stuff are so much more?" Pete said, "Well, the farmers just don't care. They wouldn't get it done if it were anymore."

I never will forget I had a horse I took up to the clinic to get castrated. Jody had just walked in from somewhere. When Pete cut off the bottom of the scrotum, he threw it at her. He said, "Honey, you always did want a horse-hide bag." Oh, never a dull moment.

Champp

Tammy Jividen

Pete was at my house to vet my horses one time. A stray cat came by and I asked Pete if he could neuter him. He said, "Yeah, sure, we'll do it right here." We had this rickety old house and I went in the backdoor, to the bathroom and I finally cornered the cat. Pete gave it a shot to tranquilize it. The cat clawed me and took up the screen door. Pete said, "Leave him alone, he'll fall down in a minute." The cat kind of slid down the screen. *Snip. Snip.* I opened the door and the old cat wallered out, never to be seen again.

Pete was our vet for many years. He vetted our three-legged dog, Tri-pod, Motley, the Dalmatian, and many horses including Stud-Muffin, Bluebeard, and Manny. Back when we started going to the Milliron Clinic, we had these crazy wild cats and they just kept having kittens and more kittens. Pete said, "If you can catch them, we can fix them." I told the girls at the clinic when we dropped them off that they were feral and to be careful. They didn't put a sign on the cage, and when they went in the next morning to get them, whichever girl it was, Pete said, "That cat came right up her front end and latched onto her head with all four claws and tore her all to pieces." Pete called them the West Virginia cats from hell. It was funny.

When we had a problem with one of our animals, we took them to the clinic. The drive from West Virginia was long; we knew we would always be there most of the day. We always took food because there was no place to eat out on State Route 550. Pete was getting ready to work on this big old Friesian mare that had some kind of windpipe problem. Oh my God, she was gorgeous. We helped them waller that horse out of the stall, onto the surgery cart, to the surgery room. After we got all that done, I told Pete, "We brought food. Can we eat now, are you done?" He said, "Yeah, go ahead and set the table." My sister, who had never been to the clinic before, said, "Where's the table?" Pete pointed, "Right there." My sister said, "The surgery table where the horse was?" Pete said, "Yeah, just wipe it off a little bit." So, we laid out the sandwiches.

I think Jody was with us the day we had to put my son's palomino, Champ, down. Champ had heaves really bad.

There used to be a drug for that, dicticide, and then they took it off the market. Before Pete came, he told me to slope a grave behind the house so we could just walk the horse down into it so it wouldn't be traumatized. We made an appointment with Pete to come within the week. It was a cold day. We put hay in the grave, walked Champ in and out several times a day, feeding him apples in the grave. Pete arrived, and we all walked the horse up to the grave. It was a five-minute walk to the grave. I asked Pete, "Did you bring the tranquilizer shot?" Pete said, "No!" Off he goes in his gumboots to the five-minute walk back to his car to get the tranquilizer. He came back and gave Champ the tranquilizer while he was eating apples. I'll never forget it. Pete was getting ready to give Champ his last shot. Pete breathed into Champ's nostril and told me something about an old Indian saying about capturing a horse's spirit that way. Then Champ went down easy.

Jody, Pete's wife, told me once there was a little short lady who came to clean the clinic stalls. Pete loved to play jokes. The woman wanted to know if Pete would wash her horse's sheath. She asked Jody if she thought Pete would do it. Jody said, "Sure, Pete will do it, go ask him." The woman walks up to Pete real quiet. Tiptoeing to Pete she said, "Would you wash my horse's winkie?" Pete cracked up. Jody said she thought he was going to roll on the barn floor.

Reflection

Rev. E. F. Michael Morgan, Ph.D.

I recall the time Pete Smith gave me, an untested 'over-east' Episcopal priest, a chance to see how things were really done out in the country. Shortly after arriving in Athens, Ohio, from historic Boston, Massachusetts (feeling as though I had left civilization behind), Pete spoke to me at an early Sunday morning service and said I was welcome to "come on out" and see him operate on a horse... *A what?* A horse....Was I interested?

I had never given much thought to the perplexity of how to anesthetize a large animal, let alone conduct delicate surgery upon one. And yet, I was struck by the care and genuine compassion Pete felt for the sick horse under the knife. Pete seemed oblivious to distractions; not at all bothered by the messy sutures, unappealing ooze, and infected sores that festered in wounds and injured body parts. My reaction was "yuck." This wasn't exactly the proverbial Sunday-drive or walk-in-the-park I anticipated; rather it was a down-to-earth guy very much in touch with nature's way; understanding biochemistry, comprehending microbiology, and exploring the mysteries of physics. His veterinary medicine was both an art and a science. Pete simply loved animals. Covered in dirt, blood, grit, medicines, pills and potions, Pete was engaged in healing God's noble creatures – *"All things bright and beautiful, all creatures great and small."*

The following Sunday in church, bright and early, after my visit to the farm, Pete was all cleaned-up, looking good, yet somewhat uncomfortable in his Sunday-best. We exchanged consecrated elements at the altar rail - not sure exactly what was going-on theologically - then he left, and passed along God's saving grace to the countless animals he held. Well done, good and faithful servant.

About the Author

From Ohio, USA, Gina McKnight is the author of children's literature and poetry. In 2017, she released three books about Dr. Smith, including *Milliron: Abbott "Pete" Smith D.V.M. The Official Biography, Tales of A Country Vet*, and the production of *The South High Horseman: Stories and Poems by a Teen Cowboy* by Peter Smith. Currently, she is a contributing columnist for *trueCOWBOYmagazine*, *Florida Equine Athlete*, and *Arabian Finish Line*. Besides a freelance writer, she is an avid blogger about her life in rural Ohio. Gina lives on her family farm with her husband, son, and American Quarter Horses Zubedia and Mac.

On the Back Cover:
Photo Courtesy of Eric and Rhonda Curfman: Dr. Pete Smith astride Unique in the highlands of Middle Mountain, West Virginia. Eric writes, "This picture was taken in 2009 on private property owned since the late 1800's by the Arborgast family. It is on the county line of Randolph and Pocahontas, looking at the head of Gandy Creek, upstream of the Sinks of Gandy. Pete and I rode on this property for the first time in 1997. When seeing it for the first time, he commented on how it reminded him of Colorado. Anytime we traveled to this area to ride, he insisted on riding to this trail at least one day. Rhonda and I think of him every time we ride up there. Pete called it God's Country."

Made in the USA
San Bernardino, CA
19 June 2017